NOBODY
but the
WIND

By Barbara Winther

Illustrated by Mikael Johnson

Old Bear Publishing

Old Bear Publishing
Copyright © 2014 Barbara Winther
All rights reserved.

ISBN: 1505367786
ISBN 13: 9781505367782

In memory of my son
David,
who walked on many Sierra trails,
and for my son
Mikael,
who carries his brother's shadow.

"You shall walk where only the wind has walked before."*

*From *This Is the American Earth,*
by Ansel Adams and Nancy Newhall

TABLE OF CONTENTS

PROLOGUE—MOVING

Eleven year old Ken Reede hunched down in the back seat as his father drove at a steady 55. "Got to remember this date," Ken mumbled to himself. "April 17, 1965, worst day of my life." He glanced at his Willy Mays watch. "And it's two o'clock. Three hours and twenty-seven minutes since my world cracked up."

"What're you muttering about?" said his brother Ian, a college freshman. He sat on the other side of the back seat. Ken's calico cat Gypsy slept between them.

"Nothing important," Ken replied, eying the granite cliffs that towered on either side of the road. They seemed to announce, *We're in charge now.*

His fingers twitched. His hands felt cold and sweaty. He rubbed them together. Pressing his nose against the window pane, he stared at the mountains and swallowed hard, fighting back a fear of what lay ahead.

He'd left behind everything he cared about—the big house in San Francisco, the park where he'd hit three home runs to the cheers of teammates— his friends, school, bedroom and half of his belongings. Here he was, being driven up into unknown mountain territory. The future— ominous.

His father, shoulders stiff like a drill sergeant, continued to drive up the highway to their new home on the crest of the Sierra. They were going there because his father had a new job. An important position, according to Ken's mother—something to do with studying mountain snow. She sat in the front passenger seat, dozing, having gotten up at dawn to take charge of which boxes and furniture would go into the moving van and what must be left on the lawn for the Goodwill truck.

This morning, after his mother had carried an arm full of dishes out to the lawn, Ken had asked her, "How come we got to get rid of so much?"

She waved a hand at a pesky fly. "Kenny, we've talked about this move for over a month. We're going from a big house to a small cabin." She briefly closed her eyes, and then sighed as if the loads were getting too heavy. "That's why you must share a loft bedroom with your brother."

"Whoa! Don't remember hearing about that."

"Maybe you weren't listening. Sometimes you get that far-away look, especially when your father's talking."

"You mean I've got to sleep in the same room as Ian?"

"Unless you'd prefer a corner of our bedroom."

Ken gulped. Either would be a disaster.

After his mother had delivered that bombshell, Ken had retreated in a daze to his room, the floor bare—his bed, dresser, desk, chair, and the few boxes of what he'd managed to save, stacked up on the front porch ready for the van. Many of his favorite things were stuck out on the lawn. Soon somebody else would own his blue and yellow lava lamp. All of the Beatle posters. The *papier mâché* lion's head he'd worn when he starred in the fifth grade play about Africa. The wooden rocking horse he'd ridden as a cowboy when he was seven. Old clothes and books his mother said were "no longer appropriate." The ten-speed bike his father told him he wouldn't need where they were going. Ken sat on his floor, knees drawn up under his chin, counting his losses, wanting to stay there forever....

But at 10 o'clock the moving van arrived. An hour later— the Goodwill truck. No option. He, too, must go.

Now in the car, Ken watched the mountains grow. He scratched Gypsy's ears. She opened her eyes, purred and went back to sleep. At least he'd been allowed to keep his cat. As long as she had a warm place to sleep, good food and her litter box, Ken knew it wouldn't matter to her where she lived. The move to the mountains was fine for Ian, too. Great, in fact. After all, hadn't he backpacked for five years? Didn't he know about high-peaks, hidden lakes, forests—all those places? At the moment, Mr. Know-It-All, with a smile on his face, was deep into a Donner Summit trail-guide.

Ken pressed his lips together and imagined himself lost in the wilderness, staggering over fallen logs, chased by a huge bear. He shivered and zipped up his parka.

Another vision appeared, this one even more frightening. He was a hundred miles from civilization, trying to scale a cliff.

Cripes, I can't make it to the top. Can't climb any more. Hands too cold. Legs won't move. It's the end of me.

He saw his body lying on a granite mountainside in a place that nobody but the wind could reach. Heard his brother say, "Too bad! Guess I should've gone with him." His mother—"If only I hadn't taken him away from San Francisco." And his father—"The poor boy never learned how to be a man."

Cut this out, he told himself, straightening his back, blinking away the terrible scene. It's not as bad as you think. Remember when you first tried to catch a ball, how Ian had laughed at you? Well, eventually you got the hang of it. Learned how to play baseball much better than Ian. It just took time. That's what you need—time.

The road was steeper now. More curves. His father slowed down. The mountains were closing in. Ken jammed his hands into his parka pockets.

"I'm going to be okay," he whispered.

Ian looked up from his guide book. "What'd you say, Kenny?"

"I said the scenery's fantastic."

"Yeah! It's even better on the Summit."

"Better?" Ken swallowed hard. "I can hardly wait."

CHAPTER 1—PLANS

(Two years later)

On the edge of a cliff crouched a ferocious cougar, ready to leap—Gypsy, perched on top of the desk, stretched, yawned and curled into a ball.

"Hey, that's not what you're supposed to do," Ken called to his cat.

She curled up tighter and slept on.

Through the open window, dusk filtered through branches of lodge-pole pines, casting a bony pattern on the loft ceiling. As he lay on his sheepskin rug, Ken stared up at the design. I'm hunkered down in a cave, he thought. Hiding. Outside, the cougar's waiting for me.

Footsteps crunched along the path in front of the cabin. Then they clumped across the porch. "Anybody home?" shouted a familiar voice at the screen door.

Ken leaped up and leaned out of his window. "How'd you get up here?" he called down to Greg, his tall, lanky friend.

"Uncle Gus had a bunch of extra Summit deliveries. He's picking me up at seven." Greg cleared his throat. "Is your brother still home?"

"Yeah. Out hiking till dinner."

"Good. Can I use his backpack? Did he give you the topo map?"

"Yeah, yeah."

"Great!"

"Not really. He said we'd probably lose the topo and ruin his pack."

Greg grimaced. "Come on, did he really say that?"

"Afraid so." Ken leaned further out the window. In the doorway stood his mother. Sunlight glinted on wisps of gray hair that strayed across her cheeks, flushed from the heat of the kitchen and the hot August afternoon. She opened the screen door and Greg slipped inside.

Two years ago, Ken had met Greg at school—the closest one in the small town of Truckee at the foot of the eastern pass. From Soda Springs, it took an hour by bus to reach it. On his first day there, Ken noticed another new student looking as lonesome and confused as he felt.

Walking over at recess, Ken introduced himself and said, "Hey man, don't worry. We'll figure things out."

"Sure hope so," was the reply.

"Want to hang around together till things improve?"

"Sounds good to me."

Greg lived in Truckee. Twice a month, on Saturdays, his Uncle Gus delivered grocery supplies to lodges in the Soda Springs area. Greg rode along with him to visit Ken for the couple of hours his uncle spent in the coffee shop. Sometimes during the week when Ian was away at college, Greg took the bus up with Ken to spend the night. When weather was good, they hiked and camped together in Summit Valley. After that first year, Ken considered Greg the best friend he ever had.

Scooting across his sheepskin rug, he raised the trap door. The pungent odor of garlic and onions wafted up. He heard Greg say, "Smells terrific, Mrs. Reede," followed by his mother's voice, "Meatloaf. Staying for supper?" and Greg's inevitable reply, "Wouldn't miss it."

A moment later Greg clambered up the ladder. His shoe caught on the edge of Ken's sheepskin. He fell with a crash that shook the rafters and sent Gypsy streaking under the bed.

Ken shut the trap door. "Welcome," he said with a grin. "Look, I'm a bobcat. "He pulled the sides of his blond hair up to look like tufted ears.

"Quit that dumb stuff," said Greg. He knelt on the sheepskin as if it was a creature to be tamed. "We need to do more planning on our trip. Where's Ian's map?"

Ken crawled over to his desk—set in the middle of the room back-to-back with Ian's—a division of territories. He rummaged through a pile of *Nature* magazines until he found the topo. Scooting over beside Greg, he spread the map out on the sheepskin.

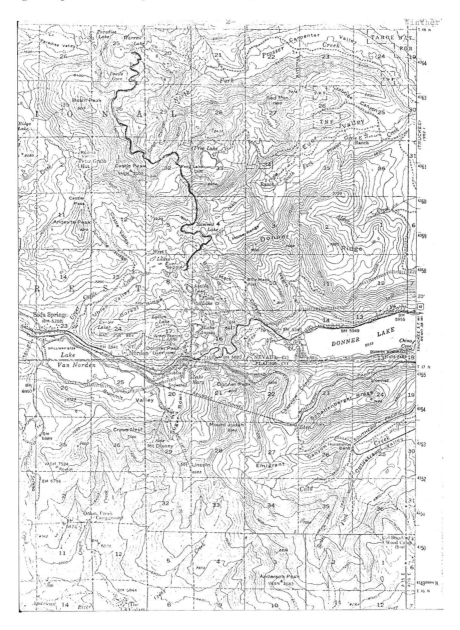

After studying it awhile, Greg said, "Just has the road from Soda down to Donner Lake. Doesn't show Interstate 80. The trail's supposed to start from it."

"Map must've been made before the highway was built."

"Yeah, must've been." Greg squinted at the topo."What do these squiggly lines mean?" He pointed. "They're real close together where we're going."

Ken shrugged. "Something to do with height, I think."

"Like what? We better find out. Can't goof up our first backpack."

"Calm down. It's not our first. Last couple of years we've camped all around Summit Valley."

"Just overnights, and some we screwed up."

Ken sat on the edge of his bed. "Okay, okay. We've got to make plans."

"Right! Don't want a disaster like that time at Yuba River."

"At least I found an old can to cook in."

"Your macaroni and cheese tasted like fish." Greg shuddered. "And we forgot the insect repellent."

"Bugs bit you bloody," Ken said, laughing.

"Not funny. And what about Kidd Lake? Woke up, our food was gone. Raccoons. Ran back to your cabin so we wouldn't starve."

"Yeah, that was bad."Ken sighed. He remembered his father's disgusted face and Ian's smirk. "But that was two years ago. We were just kids then."

"Right. So, now we're old and experienced," Greg said sarcastically. He pulled a rumpled piece of paper from his jeans pocket. "We've got to do this trip like professionals." He sat down next to Ken. "I made a checklist so we won't forget important things."

Ken took the paper and scanned the items. "What's rain gear doing on here? If it rains, we stay in the tent."

"Might want to get out, go places."

"In the rain? Why bother? Anyway, most of the time it's only an afternoon shower." Ken squinted at the list. "And why 50 feet of nylon rope?"

"If you fall over a cliff, I'll pull you up."

Ken snorted. "I won't fall over a cliff."

"Well, *I* might. Besides, we hang the food bag from a tree. Raccoons, remember?"

"Okay, okay, but you can't take your dog. Cross him off. He eats too much."

"Well, so do you." Greg grabbed the list.

Ken yanked it back and yelled, "Freeze-dried foods make people fart. And prunes? Man! You got too much on here."

"No, I don't."

"Our packs'll weigh 200 pounds."

"What're you talking about?" Greg struggled for the list.

"Now see what you did? You tore the paper."

Greg jumped to his feet and kicked the bed. "You wouldn't let go."

Gypsy hissed.

Ken did the bobcat's ears.

"You're being dumb again," Greg yelled.

"Stop calling me dumb."

"Okay, okay, so I won't take my dog, and we'll lose the prunes and rain gear, but we need everything else on this list, and you've gotta write a letter to the government."

"What for?"

"To ask what these squiggly lines mean."

"Won't get an answer by next Tuesday. Who's being dumb now?"

A loud banging shook the floor under their feet.

Ken's mother was hitting the kitchen ceiling with her broom handle. Supper was ready.

At the table, Ken dreamed about tracking the cougar across a wilderness ridge. Not until Greg asked Ian about Warren Lake did he tune into the conversation.

Ian scratched the stubble on his chin. "Sure, I've been there. Check the topo I gave Kenny. Red dot marks the best place to camp. Last mile down to the lake is really steep. Watch your feet. It's all scree and talus."

Greg said, "What's—"

Ken kicked him under the table. "My boots are good for that," he said, although he didn't know what scree and talus were either.

Mr. Reede pulled back his shoulders in a military manner. "Kenny, at your age Ian was an experienced backpacker. You still need to prove yourself."

Ken pursed his lips. "Yeah, I know. You've told me that. Several times."

His father spread his hands on the table as always when issuing wisdom. "View your first real backpacking trip as a milestone. Watch every step. Take first aid equipment as well as a book on how to use it. Before you leave, I'll check the weather report at the lab, but only use that as an indication. Air pressure and currents are unstable over high ridges. Storms can build up with very little warning."

Ian comically raised his bushy eyebrows. "Don't worry, Pop. A rescue party could reach Warren Lake in five hours, unless the weather turned catastrophic. If that happened...." He threw up his arms.

"Cut it out," Ken muttered.

"Great apricot pie!" Greg announced. "If nobody cares, I'll just eat this last piece."

Ken stopped listening. Ahead on the trail lurked the cougar, its eyes glowing like neon.

CHAPTER 2—CAROLYN

The next morning, Ken spread sunflower seeds on the stump beside the porch and called out, "Stubby."

A golden-mantled ground squirrel poked its head round the stack of firewood and then scurried for the stump. Some of its tail was gone. "Probably bitten off by a weasel," Ian had said. After Ken saw how other squirrels picked on this one, he'd started feeding it.

From the front doorway his mother called, "Kenny, a new family's moved onto the hill."

Ken returned to the porch. "Which cabin?"

"Walzac's, that barn red place." She opened the screen door and smiled.

His mother always smiled when she wanted him to do something. He didn't mind though. Jobs for his mother were never as grinding as those his father assigned.

She handed him a paper bag. "On your way to the post office, give this huckleberry jam to the new family."

Ken checked his jeans pocket. The letter he planned to mail was still there.

"The name's Jamison," his mother continued. "Tell them we'd be happy to help them get settled. They have a daughter your age. Postmaster Hart says her health's not too good."

Ken ambled off the porch and down the path. I'll visit Joe first, he thought.

"It's Jamison," his mother called after him.

"Okay," he yelled back.

He crossed the empty road and skirted a jumble of granite boulders. Stopping at the railroad tracks, he put an ear down to a rail. No humming sound. No train chugging up the mountainside. He jumped across the tracks and threaded through a stand of lodgepoles till he reached Lake Van Norden. The water level was low. Exposed snags crouched in the mud like aliens. In the moist meadow near the public campground wildflowers still bloomed—goldenrod, paintbrush, purple fireweed, and clumps of buttercups. He stood on the shore, not thinking, just feeling how it was this summer morning.

Ten minutes later he ran down the hill, swinging the paper bag, sun warming his back. When he reached the ski shop, boarded up for the summer, he slowed down. From a doorway on the other side of the parking lot, a tenor voice burst out: *"Ah! Ridi, Pagliaccio!"*—then a crash of metal—*"Sul tuo amore infranto!"*—then another crash. It was Joe, the cook at Summit Lodge Coffee Shop.

Ken peeked through the kitchen doorway. "Hi!" he said.

Joe stood in front of the iron stove, a pot lid in each hand. "Ah, Kenny, watch me make a cheese omelet for one of the train guys."

"What do cymbals have to do with it?"

"An orchestra for my omelet. Get on the perch here and help me out."

Ken set down the bag of jam and climbed up on the stool where Joe sat when he peeled vegetables. Joe handed him the lids.

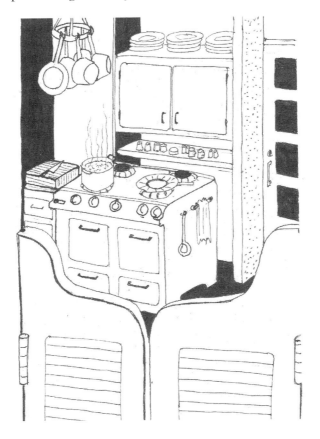

Twice a week Ken stopped in at this kitchen. Joe sang Italian opera and joked about crazy events in his life. Ken loved the singing and the stories. He relaxed with Joe, the way he always did with Old Domino—he ran the pack horse stable near Ice Lakes. And the Basque who in the summer herded his sheep up from Nevada, passing through Summit Valley, grazing in mountain pastures—in the fall, driving them down again.

Joe wiped his fat hands emphatically on his towel apron. He raised his arms and sang a piercing high G. Ken slammed the lids together.

The swinging door flew open. Velma, the ever-grumpy waitress snarled, "Where's the omelet?"

Joe pointed at the pan. "Waiting for the cheese to bubble."

"For glory sake, get it on a plate. This ain't no gourmet house." She flung back through the swinging door.

Joe shook his fist. "That woman drives me nuts." He slipped the omelet onto the plate and sprinkled it with paprika. "Only reason I work here is—the food's good." He laughed and hit the bell for Velma.

After the omelet disappeared, Ken set the lids on the potato bin and announced, "I'm going on a backpack trip with Greg. We head out at 6:00 a.m. on Tuesday. Going for three days to Warren Lake."

"Wow! Big deal for you guys."

"Sort of." Ken cleared his throat. "Joe, you're always up early. Could you give me a ride to the trailhead? It's at the top of the pass."

"Bet your life."

"Thanks. See you then."

As Ken walked up the path to the Walzac's cabin, a girl's pale face appeared in the front window. Startled, he nearly missed a porch step. Before he could knock, the front door opened, revealing a much older female face. She wore glasses and peered at him over the rims.

"Hi, I'm Ken Reede. Live up the road. I mean my family does. That is, we all do. Together."

The woman nodded. "I'm Mrs. Jamison. Please come in."

"Mom sent this huckleberry jam." He handed it to her and walked inside. "And she said if you want any help, just holler."

The girl with the pale face wore a navy blue sweatshirt that seemed to envelop her. She lifted a glass bowl off the mantelpiece and said, "Hi, I'm Carolyn. Here, have a pretzel."

He started to snatch up a handful, then thought better of it and took only one.

She gave him the bowl. "Go ahead. Take more. I don't like them much." Pushing her long, brown hair behind her ears, she walked over and sat at the table under the window.

"Okay, yeah, thanks." He couldn't stop staring at her pale skin. Never had he seen a girl with such large, dark eyes, not that he much looked at girls. He couldn't remember what the ones at school looked like. As he watched Mrs. Jamison leave the room, his stomach flip flopped and a cold wave washed through his body. The dish of pretzels seemed like a time bomb.

Carolyn said, "Well, sit down." She pointed at the chair on the other side of the table. "Push that junk out of the way. We're still getting moved in. Everything's a mess."

He eased the pretzel dish onto the table, shoved a box aside and slipped into the chair.

"Guess I got a few minutes."

"Great scenery up here," Carolyn said, looking out the window.

"Yeah, lots of trees and rocks."

She cleared her throat and gave him a sideways glance. "You got any brothers or sisters?"

"An older brother."

"That's nice."

"Not really. Thinks he knows it all. At least he's gone most of the time."

"Where to?"

"University of California. Majors in forestry."

"Good to be interested in trees."

"Yeah, I like them too."

"So, what's your father do?"

"Runs a lab. It's about snow—how high it gets, runoff—important things like that. We're all nature freaks. What've you got in your family?"

"Just my mother and father." She straightened her back. "We're up here trying things out."

"Okay," he said, wondering what *trying things out* meant.

She stared through the window. "What's that red machine up there?" She pointed.

"The chairlift for Soda Springs ski area—it's an easy slope." He wished for a glass of water. With a supreme effort he managed to swallow, gulping like a bullfrog. "Sorry."

She giggled.

His face grew warm.

"Those rocks up there"— she pointed at the ridge—"how come they're black?"

"Volcanic extrusions." He pronounced the words carefully. "At least, that's what Old Domino told me. He's my friend. Tells me things. Nature stuff, like crutose lichens. They grow on those rocks." Feeling energized, he charged on. "Something else grows up there. Can barely see it from here. It's a weird-shaped tree—a Jeffrey pine, rooted in a crack. Joe— he's another friend of mine—anyway, he climbs the ridge every year to see if it's still alive."

"I'd love to visit that weird tree."

He stood. "So, let's go."

"I can't. I'm...I'm not well enough."

He stared at her pale face. "Then let's wait till you're well."

The silence that followed was only for a minute, but Ken felt it might go on forever.

At last she looked at him and said, "Do you like plants?"

He nodded.

"Me, too. I collect wild flowers, press them in a book. Want to see— the book that is?"

He sank back into the chair. "Don't mind looking."

While Carolyn searched in another room, he finished the pretzels. He yelled, "Tons of flowers grow on the hill."

She reappeared with a blue binder, *Flowers from the Sacramento Valley* printed on the cover. "Where's the hill?" she asked.

"That's the name locals give to Donner Summit. They'd call you a flatlander."

"So, what are you? A highlander?"

He laughed. "Not sure." He touched the binder. "Big book."

She wrinkled her nose. "I'm embarrassed. You want to go?"

"I'll stay."

She wet her lips. "I'd...I'd like some new specimens—plants from around here."

"You mean wild flowers?"

"Uh huh."

"I don't pick them."

She shrugged. "Just thought maybe if you saw a bunch in a meadow, and if they weren't, you know, an endangered species, then...well...you might pick...." Her voice trailed off.

"You want to start a new collection?"

She nodded. "It'd give me something to do while I'm...while I'm getting well."

"Guess I could do that for you."

She smiled. "Know what? You're a cool highlander."

"Thanks," he croaked, then cleared his throat.

She opened the book and started showing him her pressed flowers, each with a neat label.

A while later Mrs. Jamison came back into the room.

Ken jumped up. "Got to mail a letter to the government. Promised my friend Greg I'd find out about lines on topos. Doubt if I'll get an answer by Tuesday—that's when Greg and I go backpacking—but what the heck, worth a try." He yanked open the front door, catching it before it hit the wall. "Well, I'll see you."

Halfway down the path he turned around. Carolyn still sat at the table. He waved. She waved back. When he reached the road, he raced full speed in the grass beside it. Floods of grasshoppers whirled up. Ahead an elderly lady struggled with a bag of groceries from the general store. "Hi, Mrs. Carlton," he shouted. He took her bag, opened the rear door to her car, and set it on the back seat.

"Thanks, Kenny," she called as he ran on.

Nicky, the Husky from the gas station, barked and danced around him. Ken burst into the post office, pulled the letter from his hip pocket and shot it through the mail slot. He started to dash off—

"Hold on," yelled Postmaster Hart, peering over his glasses. "What's your hurry?

Ken sang out, "I'm a cool highlander."

"Well, hurrah for you. Here, take these letters for the Snow Lab and your cabin."

Ken saluted, grabbed the pile of letters and then flew away.

Postmaster Hart shook his head in mild amusement and continued to sort the mail.

CHAPTER 3—TRAIL

The night before the backpacking trip, Ken had a hard time falling asleep. Finally, about three a.m., he dropped off.

A boom like far-away thunder pulled him awake. Vaguely, he thought a storm must be brewing. He sat up, blinked and forced himself to concentrate. Light drifted in through the branches outside the window; he could barely make out shapes in the room. His pack frame lay on the floor. Gypsy was curled up on his desk. Ian huddled under the quilt at the far end of the loft.

Again, that boom. The sound came from under his bed. He realized his mother was knocking on the kitchen ceiling with a broom handle—her signal for breakfast.

Today was the day. He leaped out of bed and charged over to his pack, jamming the nest of pans further inside so he could stuff in his parka. Gypsy disappeared under the bed. Ian poked his head out of the quilt and cried, "Quit the racket. You're a bear in a garbage can."

"I've heard worse from you," Ken yelled.

"Another one of your fantasies."

Ken considered snatching Ian's quilt and hurling it out the window. Instead, he deliberately dropped his boots. For more annoyance, he dragged his desk chair across the floor.

Ian groaned and pulled the quilt over his head.

The night before, it had taken Ken an hour to pack. He kept thinking of more things to take, not sure he had everything. What had he done with the checklist? Tossed out with the newspapers? He kept trying to picture the list in his mind.

My Sierra cup. How could I forget that? Where is it?

He remembered seeing it under the bed a week ago. Gypsy mewed plaintively as he poked through his fishing tackle and boxes of rock samples. He found the cup hooked on the tip of his deer antler.

Now, what else?

The topo map! He grabbed it from the desk and folded it. Wrong way. Unfolded it. Refolded it. No, no! One more try. There. He stuffed the map down into his pack.

Ian groaned again and flopped over to face the wall.

Ken hefted his pack, dismayed at its weight. Should he toss out the two oranges? No, they'd be great to eat. Might even offer one to Greg: *Surprise, bonehead.* He cinched his sleeping bag to the bottom of the pack frame, mentally tabulating his gear: half the food supply, plus oranges, spoon, cup, knife, cooking pans, grill rack, parka, fishhook and line, flashlight, first aid kit, map. Surely he had everything.

He reached for his billed cap and opened the trap door. In the center of the living room stood his father like a Marine sergeant. "Give me your pack," he commanded.

Ken obliged and started down the ladder.

His father examined the outside of the pack. "Where's your water bottle?"

"I, ah, I plan to get it after breakfast."

"Get it now while you're thinking about it."

"Yeah, okay." Ken scrambled back up the ladder.

At 6:05, Ken heard the horn on Joe's pickup. He grabbed a last piece of bacon, slipped his pack on, and lurched outside, chewing up the bacon as if it might save his life. He deposited the pack in the truck bed, climbed in beside Joe. and they jolted down the road.

Ahead lay Carolyn's cabin. Ken said, "Toot the horn."

Joe screwed up his face. "Why we got to do that?"

"For a friend." He waved at the cabin.

Joe pushed two beeps on his horn.

Ken pictured Carolyn's fragile hands pressing the flowers he'd taken over yesterday.

Joe whipped the truck onto Interstate 80, nearly empty this early in the day. Opening his window, he blasted into an operatic aria: *"Fra poco a me ricovero dara negletto vello."*

"Man, that's great," Ken said. "What's it mean?"

"Wild flowers soon will shed their bloom around my sad and lonely tomb."

"Wish I hadn't asked."

Joe laughed. "It's from an opera by Verdi."

"How come most of your songs have gloomy words?"

"The sadder the meaning, the better the music. Beauty can make you cry. Course it's not the same crying as when life turns you upside down. Those are different tears."

"But you're always happy," said Ken.

"Got to act that way." Joe shifted gears on the steep grade to the summit. "When I get down in the dumps, I don't throw it on people. Instead, I sing. That's my medicine."

"You get down in the dumps?"

"Yeah, sometimes my soul gets way down there."

Ken's eyes widened. "Really?"

"Bet your life." Joe thumped his chest. "Tremendous soul in here. How else you think I cook so good?" He broke into the aria with fresh vigor.

"Man, you can really sing."

Soon they reached the Summit Rest Area, jammed with overnight vehicles—trucks, RVs, and vans. In a camper doorway a blonde woman sat drinking coffee. Joe leaned out his window and shouted, "Magnificent morning!" The woman smiled and raised her cup in acknowledgement. He kissed his fingers and threw them to the sky.

Greg was sitting on a picnic table. He jumped down and ran toward them, a worried look on his face. "Tons of people waking up. Soon it'll be a madhouse. Can't find the trailhead. Uncle Gus dropped me off ten minutes ago. You're late. Where've you been?"

"Relax." Ken lifted his pack out of the truck bed. "Ian said the trail starts behind the bathrooms."

With a grunt, Joe pulled his stocky body out of the truck. I made chocolate cookies for you guys," He reached behind the seat. "Sugar ruins your teeth, but it'll help you climb like mountain goats."

"Thanks, Joe." Ken stuffed the cookies into one of the side pockets on his pack.

"Glad to contribute. Now I'm off to feed a bunch of hungry train-track workers. Kenny, when you finish your hike, call me on the pay phone." He nodded at the nearby booth. "I'll drive up and get you."

Greg said, "Can I get a ride, too? Uncle Gus wants to pick me up at Ken's."

"Bet your life." Joe swung into the driver's seat. "Have fun. "Leaning out the window, he said to Greg, "Hey, big guy, careful with your feet." He zoomed his truck around the end of a large van and disappeared down the highway.

Ken picked up two sticks and hid them behind his back, "Longest stick'll be the trail leader?"

Greg picked the longest. Ken followed him onto the trail. Birds warbled and flew around the branches of the lodgepole forest. The air smelled sweet from pink spiraea, and the pine-needled ground was wet and shiny with dew. Where the sun reached through trees, steam hung like strips of gauze. The trail dipped slightly then rose as they entered a flat space surrounded by granite boulders.

Greg called over his shoulder, "Watch out for snakes. Uncle Gus says they're under rocks."

A moment later, Ken grabbed Greg's arm.

"Snake?" gasped Greg.

"No, sh-h-h. Look on that ledge near the fallen tree."

Three animals the size of house cats were sunning themselves near a hole under a log.

"What are they?" Greg whispered.

"Marmots. Old Domino, that guy at the horse corral, showed me pictures of them."

Motionless, the marmots stared at them. Then one raised its nose and made a whistling sound. Abruptly the three disappeared.

"Awesome," said Greg, and he plodded on.

The trail grew steeper, leading them into a forest where sunlight shot rays between branches. Reaching a stream in a glen, they stopped to drink from their bottles.

Ken knelt and splashed water on his face. On the bank grew pink and yellow columbines, shooting stars and purple asters with glowing yellow centers. On the far side of the stream rose spikes of lavender flowers shaped like tiny elephant heads. "On my way back, I'll pick some for Carolyn," he murmured.

19

"Who's Carolyn?" Greg asked.

Ken flushed. He hadn't meant to say his thoughts. "Just a new girl on the hill," he said, rising, retying his green nylon wind shirt onto the frame and adjusting his pack straps. He wondered if Greg's shoulders hurt as much as his. The heavy stuff was divided; Greg carried the tarps, tent, and rope. All divided except for his oranges. More weight. Should he have left them behind?

They walked on till the forest ended and they entered a meadow of corn lilies.

"Fork ahead," said Greg. "Check the map so we know which way to go."

"Take the trail to the right," said Ken.

"How do you know?"

"It's headed for the ridge."

"Get out the topo," Greg insisted.

"No, it's stuffed down in my pack."

"Your brother said topos go in the outside flap."

Ken frowned. "I was in a hurry this morning. I'll get it later. Take the right fork."

"Thought I was the leader."

"You are, so get going."

An hour later the trail ended at a marshy pond full of mosquitoes. Attempting to make a joke of his mistake, Ken said, "Place smells like an outhouse."

Greg slopped on insect repellent. "I'll never listen to you again. You think you know everything. Well, you don't know beans."

Ken yelled back. "Look, I'm sorry."

Greg stalked past him and down the trail.

They marched back to the fork in silence.

By mid morning they reached the first crest. Before them stretched an enormous bowl. On the southern side, the trail shot up and down over jagged contours laced with ribbons of water. Wildflowers spilled across the bowl—purple, red, yellow. Carolyn would like this, Ken thought.

"Time for a break," said Greg, sinking down on the crest under a dwarf pine. It was the first time he'd spoken since the marsh.

Ken slipped off his pack and collapsed between clumps of red heather and woolly buckwheat. A few snow patches were left in shaded hollows. He pulled the dark blue bandanna from his back jeans pocket, wiped the sweat from his face, and then burrowed into his pack for the topo. With a flourish, he transferred it to the outer flap.

Greg grinned. "Smart move." He took a swig of water from his bottle. "Great view from here." He pointed. "We can even see Mt. Lincoln."

"Yeah!" Ken rubbed his sore shoulders. Again he rooted in his pack. "Want an orange?" he asked, triumphantly showing one.

"No, I'll eat a hunk of my jerky."

For the rest of the morning Ken trudged along behind Greg, the trail up and down, up and down. He tried to forget how much his shoulders ached. Tried to forget how good jerky tasted, his share left on the kitchen table. He wondered what else he'd forgotten.

Finally at noon they stopped beside a stream in a small glen. Greg produced crackers, ham, cheese, pickles and a small tube of mustard. "Want some?"

"Thanks," Ken said casually, taking a piece of cheese. "Here, have one of Joe's cookies."

A half-hour's rest and they hit the trail again, Castle Peak at their backs. Soon they came to a field of tall yellow and purple flowers. Greg said, "What's that buzzing?"

"Sounds like motorboats," said Ken.

As they drew near to the field, the buzzing increased.

"It's bees," yelled Greg. "Billions. In the flowers. Got to detour."

"How?" Ken pointed to the cliff that shot up a sheer hundred feet on one side and then hooked his thumb at the steep drop-off that edged the other.

Greg blinked. "Well, we can't cross this field. We'll get stung."

"We've got long-sleeve shirts and our legs are covered. Pull out a jacket or something to hide your face. Bees are after flowers, not us." Ken chewed on his lower lip. "Look—we've got three choices—stay here, go home, or walk through the field. As for me, I'm plowing on through." He untied his nylon wind shirt and covered his head except for his eyes. He shoved his hands into his jeans pockets and waded in. Purple and yellow flowers reached as high as his waist. All he could see were multitudes of yellow and black bugs flying around him. As he moved forward, their buzzing increased in volume.

"You're gonna get stung," Greg yelled after him.

"Then I'll swell up and die," Ken shouted back, his voice muffled by the wind shirt. "You'll have to dig a hole and bury me."

"Not funny."

The buzzing increased around Ken's head and shoulders as if the field were filled with power saws. Slowly he swiveled his head, relieved to see Greg following but amused at how he looked—red parka over his head, gloves on his hands, arms straight out—like a zombie. Ken reached the middle of the field, then heard a screech. He whipped his head around. Greg was gone. In one place, bees spun higher. "Greg?" he yelled, starting back.

Greg struggled to his feet, bees swirling around him. "Hit a patch of mud."

"You okay?"

"Yeah. Didn't even get stung."

Relieved, Ken continued forward, careful of his footing. When he reached the end of the field, he didn't look back, afraid he might put a hex on Greg's progress.

At last Greg staggered out, fell to his knees and kissed the ground. Ken laughed, yanked off his wind shirt, and retied it to his pack frame.

"Feel as if I can do anything," Greg announced, stuffing his parka back into his pack.

Ken said, "Good, 'cause check out the trail ahead. Looks tough."

Four switchbacks angled up the steep mountainside.

They started the climb, pausing at each turn, breathing hard. At last they reached the saddle. Nestled below on the other side was Warren Lake, so far down it appeared the size of a swimming pool. According to the map, what looked like dot in the middle of the lake was really an island.

Ken wiped the sweat from his neck and studied the terrain between them and the lake—a steep swath of loose rocks about ten-foot wide. "No trail down," he said to Greg.

"Right, well, I don't want to be the leader any more. You go first."

Ken inched down sideways, balancing with his arms, placing his feet carefully. With each step small piles of rock crackled down the slope like buckshot on a tin roof—*scree and talus,* he realized. As he descended, he grasped boulders, roots, and small tree trunks. At one point he lost his balance and started to slide but shoved his heels into the rocks and grabbed a wiry shrub that cut his hand. A stream of scree and talus clinked on down. "How're you doing?" he yelled back at Greg.

"Okay, I guess."

Ken passed slabs of stone fractured from the mountainside. A lizard darted across his path. A squirrel on a rock chirred and flicked its tail. Slowly, the lake grew larger and larger. Three quarters of the way down, the slope leveled, but then steepened again. Carefully, Ken crunched on down to the bottom. Before him, the lake spread like a huge, oval, royal-blue mirror. For a minute he stood on the shore, staring, breathing it in. Then he unbuckled his pack and dropped it onto the rock-strewn ground. Feeling light as a bird, he yanked off his boots and flung away his clothes. With a wild yell, he plunged into the icy water, collapsed onto his back and spouted streams at the sky.

Sliding the last few feet down the slope, Greg hollered full blast—"I made it. I made it."

Ken whopped in reply.

Their voices echoed against the stone cliffs.

CHAPTER 4—CAMPSITE

The lake was surrounded by tall granite cliffs, broken only by a narrow Prosser Creek Canyon at the northeast end and a steep swath of loose rock on the eastern side, where the boys had come down. Along the flat shoreline, large boulders rose between pine trees and shoulder-high shrubs. Ian had told them the best campsite was near a spring at the south end of the lake. After a rest, they headed that way.

Ken stopped in a cove. "Hey, man," he called to Greg. "Here's an old boat."

Greg peered under the branches where a dinghy was partially hidden. "Wonder how it got here?"

Ken surveyed the cliffs. He pointed north. "Must of come through that way. That's where the topo showed a stream enters the lake. Nobody could've carried it down the way we got here."

Greg examined the bottom. "Someone's tried to seal the crack."

Ken sniffed the repair. "Pine pitch. Smells fresh."

Greg glanced around. "Don't like the idea of strangers lurking."

They continued along the shore till they reached a small stream, following it up about twenty feet to the spring. Behind it, three slabs of granite that looked like wide steps led to a dense tangle of growth. The bushes thinned to a jumble of rocks at the foot of the cliff. In two nearby pines, a group of Cassin's finches announced their arrival and then swarmed away into the graying sky.

They camped in a flat area of coarse gravel. After gathering scraps of wood and building a fire, Ken set the grill on top and heated a pan of water to cook their freeze-dried stroganoff. Meanwhile, Greg spread the tarp on the ground, set out the mats and unrolled the sleeping bags.

As Ken emptied the stroganoff packet into the boiling water, he thought he heard something—a rustle in the growth above the granite slabs. Hoping it was just his imagination, he straightened up and listened, clutching the packet over the pan. For a moment he heard only the bubbling stroganoff. Then the rustle came again, unmistakable this time.

"Something's in the bushes," he whispered to Greg who knelt beside him.

"I heard it."

"Ouch!" Ken yanked his hand away from the pan and blew on his fingertips.

Greg moved closer to the fire. "Sounded like a big animal."

"Could be a cougar." Ken mentally measured the distance to the two pine trees. "I'll take the right. You take the left."

"Left what?" squeaked Greg.

"Tree, bonehead." Ken crawled to his pack and searched the side pockets till he found his Swiss Army knife. The feel of it gave him confidence. "Could be a bear."

"Bears climb trees," said Greg.

"So do cougars." Ken considered bolting for the lake.

Ten minutes passed with no further sounds. Ken slipped the knife into his jeans and returned to the stroganoff, now stuck to the bottom of the pan. "Whatever it was, it's gone."

"Gone, " Greg echoed.

Ken laughed in an evil manner and hunched his shoulders menacingly. "But who knows what prowls in the dark night."

"Cut that out." Greg tossed another stick on the fire. "We ought to hang up our food."

"Here, eat your dinner first." Ken handed over Greg's Sierra cup full of stroganoff. "It's a bit scorched."

"Is there a moon tonight?" Greg asked hopefully.

"Don't know. Even if there is, with all these high cliffs we might not see it. Come on, eat your dinner before it gets cold."

They ate in silence, neither mentioning the burned taste. After dinner, Greg hurled his rope over a tree limb and started to hang up their food bag. Then he froze.

A rock the size of a baseball was falling over the edge of the top granite slab. It landed with a metallic clack-clack onto the middle slab. Then it clattered on down to the bottom, stopping not far from their sleeping bags.

Ken whipped out his knife and crouched. But the blade wouldn't open. Rusted shut.

"Holy cripes!" he muttered.

A gravely crunch issued from the bushes above the slabs.

With a shriek, Greg dropped the food bag and ran for the left tree.

More crunches, louder.

"It's attacking!" Ken bellowed. He jammed his knife back into his pocket, rushed for the tree on the right, and swung up.

From his second limb Greg wailed, "The food, the food! I didn't hang it up."

Ken shouted, "You're so smart with your lists and plans. Now, what'll you do about it?"

"Well, since you're so brave, climb down, get the bag, and hand it up to me."

Ken rubbed his hands together, sticky with pine pitch that smelled like turpentine. "That's not a good idea," he said.

The sky darkened. The lake turned black. The fire died out. They continued to sit in the trees.

"I'm cold," said Greg, "and I'm hungry."

"We ate dinner."

"Wasn't much. I'd like a candy bar."

Ken found himself considering how good his orange would taste. "Don't think about it," he said, shifting his body, trying to find a comfortable position. A snag from a broken limb pushed into his ribs, so he leaned forward, but that made him feel giddy and unbalanced. He reached above to a small branch covered with rough bark and looped an arm around it.

Cougars or bears wouldn't make all that noise, he concluded. A person had done it. Not a robber. If it were then the falling rock would've been accidental and after that a thief would've stayed quiet. Instead, all that crashing. Somebody wanted to scare them, let them know they were being watched. But why?

He flinched as bats feeding on insects flapped in over the campsite.

Gradually the sky to the east lightened. Although the moon didn't appear over the ridge, the tops of the western cliffs glowed with an eerie, blue light.

"Greg whispered," Lake's sure in a deep hole."

"Yeah. Moon could rise and set and we'd never see it." Ken switched arms over the upper branch.

Suddenly, the air split with a series of yips and howls that reverberated in chilling echoes, bouncing against the rocky cliffs, back and forth.

"Coyotes," Ken said in a voice full of awe.

Then the night was quiet again except for the spring gurgling, the crickets chirping, and the water lapping against the lakeshore.

"I'm staying up here all night," said Greg.

"You'll go to sleep and fall out."

"I'll tie myself to the trunk."

Ken snickered. "Your rope's on the food bag."

"I'll wedge myself in."

"If we don't get a fire going soon, we'll be surrounded by coyotes." Ken growled for effect.

"Quit that. You know it's not true."

"Then let's get out of the trees. "

"No."

"But I've got a kink in my neck, my back aches and this pitch is sticky. Besides, haven't heard anything for over an hour."

"You go down first," Greg suggested.

"No way. Both of us go down together."

"When?"

"In five minutes," said Ken.

"Can't see my watch."

"We'll count out loud to two hundred and then climb down."

There was no reply.

"Okay?" insisted Ken.

Greg sighed. "Okay."

They counted in unison, starting off loudly and ending in a whisper.

"All right," said Ken, unhooking his arm from the branch. "Let's go."

They climbed down and Ken ran to build up the fire. "Not enough wood for the night," he yelled.

Greg groaned. "Well, I'm not hunting in the dark."

"At least hang up the food."

"Right!" Cautiously, Greg approached the food bag, glanced around, and then pulled it up three quarters of the way to the limb, tying the end of the rope around the tree trunk. He stiffened. "What was that?"

"Just a frog. Relax."

"I'd feel better if I could see the moon."

"Look!" Ken yelled.

"Where?" Greg yelped.

"Up there. A meteor just streaked the sky. Joe says that means a witch has died. Man, there goes another one."

"Cut it out. I don't want to hear any more about meteors and witches. And don't yell unless there's an emergency."

Ken shrugged. He stepped back from the fire to stare at the sky. "Just think, those stars'll be there after we've died."

"Don't want to hear about dying either. Let's set up a night watch. Three-hour shifts. Since I'm wide awake, I'll go first. You go to bed, so you'll be ready."

"Still think you're the leader?"

"Somebody's got to take charge." Greg pulled on his red parka, yanked on his gloves, and stretched his wool cap down over his ears. He hauled his mat and sleeping bag over to the left tree, crawled into the bag and drew it up around his shoulders. Then he propped himself against the trunk, his flashlight beside him.

"You look ready for anything," Ken said.

"Go to sleep."

Ken took off his boots, climbed into his sleeping bag, and zipped it up. Lying on his back, he smelled the freshness of pines and listened to all the sounds—the stream, the crickets, and an occasional plop in the lake—a fish or frog. As he surveyed the sky and the moon's reflection on the southern cliff, Carolyn slipped into his mind. He imagined her pressing flowers in her book. He saw her eyes, heard her voice, and wondered what kind of sickness kept her from hiking. Would she like sleeping outside? He thought she would. Everyone ought to have a chance to sleep under the stars.

It was getting cold. Turning on his side, Ken slid further into his flannel-lined bag. Greg's snores sounded like a train chugging up a mountain. Some watchman!

Remembering the times they'd camped together in Summit Valley, Ken thought about the few dumb decisions they'd made. Not all bad. Hadn't they solved problems? Yeah. Greg hadn't acted afraid then. Maybe that was because those trips were just overnights, close to home. And maybe—because his parents and brother had still been alive.

After they died last winter in a car crash, Greg never tackled anything new. Lucky his uncle stepped up and gave him a home. Even though the old guy was a grump with fierce eyes and a chin that jutted out when he talked, you could tell he cared about Greg.

To Ken, the most important thing in life was a home base. Even when he fantasized about running away, he knew he'd miss the cabin, the loft, his mother, his friends.

Maybe he wouldn't miss his father and brother, but then maybe he would. Certainly he didn't want them to die. No wonder Greg was easily frightened.

He glanced over at his friend, propped up against the tree, sound asleep, looking like an overstuffed scarecrow. Greg was a good dude. A loyal friend. Not fair to poke fun at his fears.

Ken stared at the rock steps, the bushes, the cliff, wondering who had watched them—and why. The spring gurgled. A frog croaked. He was warm now. His eyes closed.

CHAPTER 5—DISCOVERY

The next thing Ken knew, it was daylight and sun blasted over the corner of Prosser Creek Canyon, warming the air. Greg, still propped against the tree trunk, snored like a locomotive.

"Get wood," Ken shouted, leaping from his sleeping bag and sprinkling pine needles on the few remaining coals. He blew fiercely. "Some watchman you are! You never woke me up."

"So what?" Greg staggered to his feet with a groan. He flexed his fingers and rolled his shoulders. "One look at me must've frightened them away."

Ken laughed. "Sure, whatever."

After breakfast a Clark's nutcracker flew into camp and eyed the site, protesting the lack of food with a harsh *char-r-ring* sound. Ken tossed his remaining bread crust at the bird. As he doused the remnants of their fire with water, he said to Greg, "Want to explore the area above the granite slabs?"

"No!"

"It's not scary this morning."

"Forget it. I'm not going."

Ken stared at the mass of bushes, surprised at how they could grow out of such a steep mountainside. He squinted up higher and then said, "Smoke. Bet it's a campsite."

"Where?"

Ken pointed. A faint wisp curled out of the cliff, scarcely visible against the trees and gray rock.

"Dumb place to camp," Greg said.

"Must be a reason." Ken started up the granite slabs. "I'm checking it out."

Greg yelled, "Come back."

"You don't have to come with me."

With a groan, Greg clambered up the granite after Ken. "Can't let you go alone."

Near the west end of the top slab, Ken found a faint path leading through the maze of bushes. He pointed to the trampled sedge still green. "Look, it's been used." Brushing aside the whitethorn, he started up the path through a heavy thicket, ducking under and climbing over limbs. In a pocket ahead grew elderberries and tall willows. Greg followed, huffing as the mountainside steepened.

Suddenly, sharp, bleating *"inks"* issued from a mass of boulders. Ken pointed to a furry, guinea pig-like creature on a rock. "A pika," he said. "Old Domino told me what it sounds like."

After a pause, Ken moved on more slowly, at a pace Greg could handle. Finally, the path ended in layers of rock and scattered red firs.

Smoke rose from a split in a large, flat rock. Ken said softly, "Must be a cave under there."

"Don't want to know about it."

"Won't hurt to look." Ken dropped to his knees and began to crawl forward.

"We might get mistaken for animals," Greg whispered. "Might get shot."

"Hog wash!" Ken reached the smoking hole, peeked in, tried to stifle a cough and turned away. "Can't see anything. Too smoky."

Greg said, "Let's go back now."

Ken shook his head. Flattening his body, he scooted across the granite to the edge of the rock and peered over. Below him was the mouth of a cave, fronted by a narrow ledge. Firs, rising from a pocket of ground below, branched out so the cave could not be seen from the lake.

Beneath the firs, a sheer cliff fell about 30 feet. There were no sounds from inside the cave. The only way to reach it was by way of rock footholds wedged into a crevasse on the right side.

Greg crawled up beside him and looked over. "What're you going to do?" he whispered.

"Explore the cave."

"Might be a bear in there."

"Bears don't build fires."

"Then, a hermit."

"Yeah," Ken said, "a loony with a long beard."

"Quit that."

"Sh-h-h, not so loud. Probably a camper who likes to be alone."

"Then, leave him alone," said Greg.

"I'm checking out the cave. Stay here if you want."

As Ken climbed down the crevasse, the air grew deadly quiet. Even grasshoppers quit rasping. He reached the ledge and edged toward the opening. Holding his breath, he peeked inside. Slowly letting out his breath, he stepped in, squinting into the cave.

Greg called down, "Anybody in there?"

Ken returned to the entrance and called up. "Nope."

"I'm coming down." Greg plunged noisily into the crevasse, sending loose rocks over the cliff.

Ken cringed. "Holy cripes, you're loud!'"

"Well, you coughed at the smoke hole."

"You made more noise."

Ken bent over and re-entered the cave, Greg behind him.

The cave extended back a good eight feet, with a ceiling too low to stand up and a width slightly more than the sleeping bag stretched out lengthwise at the far end. Scattered over the floor were fruit pits, empty cans, crumpled foil and plastic wrappers. About a quarter ways back, embers of a fire were sending smoke up through a black-ringed slit in the roof.

As their eyes grew accustomed to the dimness, they saw food supplies piled up against the walls: smoked fish, three packages of marshmallows, a carton of oatmeal, a jar of honey, envelopes of powdered milk, a can of vegetable oil, and little bags of dried fruit—prunes, apricots, raisins.

On a wooden peg pounded into a fissure on the sloping back wall hung a grimy khaki shirt. Across one corner, looped a tree root that had forced its way through a ceiling crack. Hooked over the root was a double roll of salami, and beneath it, a pile of clothes. Strewn around the fire were dirty cooking utensils. And everywhere—ants.

"What a garbage dump!" said Greg. He lifted the wooden lid from a tall, square can next to the fire, sniffed the interior, and dipped in a finger to taste it. "It's water."

Ken pointed at soot drawings of girls on the ceiling. "Not prehistoric," he said with a laugh.

Pebbles clattered down on the outside ledge. Greg grabbed Ken's arm. "Somebody's coming."

Soft scraping sounds in the crevasse.

Greg hid behind the khaki shirt. Ken, mesmerized, stared at the front of the cave.

Out on the ledge appeared the silhouette of a man.

"Holy cripes," Ken breathed.

The man bent over and entered. He stopped at the fire, lifted the lid from the square can, cupped his hand inside and drank, flicking off excess drops that sizzled on the coals. Looking around in the dim light, he met Ken's eyes and froze. Then, with a growl, he grabbed a stick of wood and crouched as if to attack.

Ken cowered. He felt like a cornered rabbit about to be eaten. His stomach gurgled.

The man swore and sank down. He leaned against the wall and, still holding the stick, glared at the intruder.

In the fire's faint glow, Ken could see the man's face was thin. His streaked blonde hair hung to his shoulders. He wore a green shirt several sizes too big and a beat-up suede vest.

"What're you doing here, kid?" the man growled. "How'd you find my cave?"

"Saw the smoke," Ken replied in a husky voice. "We followed the path."

"We?"

"Me and Greg." Ken hooked his thumb over his shoulder.

The stranger leaned forward and peered into the darkness. "What's he doing behind my khaki shirt?"

"Hiding,"

The stranger snorted.

Greg cleared his throat and crawled onto the sleeping bag. He sat there, blinking like a barn owl.

In the silence that followed, Ken noted the stranger had only a faint stubble of a beard, odd for a man holed up in a cave. Studying his face, the realization hit him—he's not much older than me—sixteen at the most. He blurted out, "Did you watch us last night?"

"Yeah."

"How come?"

The older boy didn't answer.

A snap burst from the fire.

Greg let out a yelp.

Ken stiffened.

"How long you camping at the lake?" the older boy asked.

"Two more nights," said Ken.

The older boy wrinkled his nose. "I don't want you kids hanging around."

"We'll stay out of your way." Ken rose. "Come on, Greg."

"Sit down!" The older boy waved them back. "You shouldn't've come. Don't like snoopers."

"We weren't snooping," said Ken. "Just came for a quick look."

"Can we go now?" Greg asked.

"Maybe I won't let you go at all," said the older boy with a sneer. "How about that?"

"Why keep us here?" Greg asked, his voice rising an octave.

"I might tie you up. Let you starve."

Ken said quickly, "Thought you didn't want us hanging around."

The older boy's eyes narrowed. His body seemed bigger with the silence. "If I let you go, you'll tell."

"About what?" Ken whispered. Sweat trickled down his back as if his body had sprung a leak.

"About me in this cave."

"We won't tell, honest," squeaked Greg

"Why don't you want anybody to know?" Ken ventured.

"None of your business. Plan to squeal on me?"

Greg said, "I swear I'll never talk to anybody...about anything...ever."

The older boy poked at the fire with his piece of wood. It blazed up.

With difficulty, Ken swallowed. He tried to keep his voice steady and friendly. "I'm Ken. This dude here's Greg. What's your name?"

No answer.

Ken persisted. "Been living in the cave long?"

"What's it to you?"

"Just wondering."

The older boy continued to poke at the fire. "I'm staying here a year."

"Through the winter?" Ken was shocked.

"Sure."

"What'll you eat?"

"Trap squirrels, smoke fish."

Ken shook his head. "Squirrels hibernate. The lake'll freeze over."

"I'll dig the animals out." The older boy flourished the smoking stick. "See all the food I got here? Most of it left behind by campers. I'll have a cave full by first snowfall."

"You're nuts," Ken said.

The older boy leaned forward in a menacing way. "Watch it, kid."

Ken sputtered on, "How're you going to keep warm in blizzards? At this altitude you'll freeze. Where're you from, anyway?"

"No place," the older boy shouted, half rising. "Look, if you tell about me, I'll find a way to cut out your tongues and pickle them." He yanked another piece of wood from the fire and brandished both flaming sticks at them. "Now get out. Both of you. Hear me? Now!"

Ken and Greg bolted toward the mouth of the cave and along the ledge, Greg balancing dangerously on the precipice. They scrambled up the crevasse as if pursued by a cougar.

"Creepy kids," the older boy shouted up the smoke hole. "You're just a couple of creeps."

Ken charged down the mountain, scarcely aware of thorny branches or whether Greg was behind him. Finally he reached the camp and sank down, breathing hard, dripping with sweat. He focused on his boots to steady himself. He envisioned Caveman staggering up to the Reede cabin and bellying across the front porch, begging for food. Then he saw him encased in a block of ice.

Gradually, the world took shape again. Finches warbled. Sunlight lit up the island in the lake. The water, like a looking glass, reflected the trees and boulders along the shore. Beside him sat Greg, armpits smelling like skunk cabbage. Ken stood up. "Caveman is a weirdo."

"Right," Greg agreed.

A chipmunk, exploring Ken's pack, leaning against his tree, slipped and fell into the empty cooking pot. Squeaking frantically, it clawed at the metal sides until Ken turned the pot on its side. The chipmunk scurried to the rocks where it flicked its tail and chattered annoyance. "Next time," Ken told it, "be careful what you investigate." He set the pot upright. "Me, too," he added and kicked a pine cone for emphasis.

"Come on, Greg," he said, "let's do something different." He dug into his pack and brought out a plastic bag that held a fish line, two hooks, and a sinker.

Greg retrieved the topo map. "Caveman called us creeps. Well, he's a bigger one."

"Yeah, but he ought to leave that cave before winter." Ken managed to pull a blade out of his pocket knife. He found a nearby thin willow branch and tried sawing it off. Finally, the branch broke; he tested its strength for a fishing pole.

Greg studied the map. "Just over the ridge is Devil's Oven Lake."

"So?"

"So let's go over there and set up camp. Got to get out of here."

"We can't scale that cliff. Besides, Ian said it's even steeper going down. Look, while I'm fishing, check out Prosser Creek."

"Why?"

"See if any campers are there."

Greg frowned. "What if I meet Caveman?"

"Ignore him. He'll probably ignore you. I wouldn't go near that old boat, though. Probably his." Ken started for the shore. "And when you get back," he shouted over his shoulder, "take a swim, man. You stink.

That night, Ken fried the trout he'd landed in the afternoon with the willow pole. He figured the fish was about 12 inches long. "No big deal," he said to Greg who was impressed. "I've landed larger ones from the lake at home."

The truth was he'd only caught a few fish before and none of them this big. Also, he didn't tell Greg about nearly losing it. When he jerked the line ashore, the trout flew off the hook. Took him ten minutes to find it in the bushes.

After supper they sat around the fire blowing Beatle tunes on paper-covered combs. When the coyotes yipped, Greg jumped to his feet. This time, however, he didn't yell and head for a tree. He even managed a grin when Ken howled back an answer.

As night settled in, they pulled their sleeping bags close to the fire. It grew so cold even the crickets stopped singing.

"No need to stand a watch," said Ken. "Caveman's seen enough of us."

CHAPTER 6—STORM

The early morning sky was brilliant. Reds, purples and golds exploded from the east, spilling into the south. Ken sat up, humped over in his sleeping bag, blowing white breath into the icy air, as he watched the sky lighten and fog swirl over the lake.

From the trees on the western side a bird chirped, answered by a lower call. Then the morning was quiet. It seemed as if everything was waiting for the sun. At last it inched over the crest—a glowing ball of instant warmth, greeted by a chorus of birds—and the noisy Clark's nutcracker flew back into the campsite, demanding food.

The boys spent the morning exploring the lake's western and south-ern shores, searching for a campsite away from the granite slabs. The day before, Greg had spotted a good place at the start of Prosser Canyon—but now when he led Ken there, a man was setting up camp. With him were two boys who looked about eight years old.

"What do you want?" the man asked belligerently.

"Nobody was here yesterday," Greg said. "Thought we'd check out the campsite."

"It's a lousy one," snapped the man. "But I've hiked up this stupid canyon until my legs feel like rubber and these kids are bellyaching and I've got to set up this dumb tent and I'm not going anyplace else. Don't know how I got talked into this idiotic camping trip."

"Mom said it would be fun," said one of the boys.

"I'm starved," said the other.

"Sorry to bother you," said Ken. "We're camped at the other end of the lake."

"Good," said the man. "Thomas, put down that jar of peanut butter."

There was the crash of a bottle breaking.

"Now look at what you've done," yelled the man. "Don't step in it. Get away, for God's sake."

One of the boys burst into tears. The other one said, "Can we lick up the peanut butter?"

Ken and Greg hurried past.

"Better stay where we are," Ken said.

They returned to their camp for lunch. Afterwards, they skipped stones across the lake's surface and gathered wood for the night fire. Then, in the heat of mid afternoon, they left their clothes on a sandbar and swam to the island and back.

Ken pointed to a log on the edge of the lake. "Help me float it?"

"Looks heavy."

"Let's try."

After a struggle, prying and shoving, they succeeded.

Ken climbed astride. "I'm Lord Nelson," he cried, splashing his feet through the water, attempting to navigate. He pointed to a yellow-legged frog peering up from the cattails. "Napoleon off the starboard bow."

"That's kid stuff," said Greg's

"So what?" Switching onto his stomach, arms loose in the water, Ken let the log drift out into the lake. He lay there, relaxed, sun beating hard on his back.

Gradually, a shadow spread north across the water. Clouds like chunks of coral crept in from the south, and a gust of wind sent ripples northward. Noticing the change, Ken tried to paddle toward the sandbar but made no progress. He sat up, kicked the water with his feet, then bent over and thrashed with his arms and legs. Still, the lopsided log stayed in the same place.

Again the wind gusted.

Greg yelled, "Better come back."

Ken didn't want to abandon the log. Another look at the sky, though, told him he had no other choice. Dark clouds were barreling in. He slipped off the log and started to swim for the sandbar. The wind increased, pushing waves against him. For a few fearful moments he couldn't see the shore. Then came a crack of intense light followed by a clap of thunder, echoing back and forth from the cliffs.

"Hurry up!" cried Greg.

Ken swam faster, harder, adrenaline pumping. Don't panic, he told himself. One, two, breathe. One, two, breathe....

It seemed he'd been swimming forever. Waves getting bigger, wind blowing harder. What if his muscles gave out? Keep calm, take breaths, he told himself. Then at last, shallow water. He staggered ashore. Hands shaking, he pulled on his shirt, jeans, and boots. "Get the rain gear?" he gasped.

"Didn't bring it. You said we wouldn't need it."

Three more lightning flashes struck in quick succession. Thunder blasted like a shot from a cannon.

In camp, the wind had ripped Greg's parka from the top of his pack. He found it under a bush. The food bag swung like a pendulum. Cooking utensils and supplies were scattered. Ken yelled, "Get the tarp." He ran to lower the food bag and struggled with the stiff rope fibers to untie the knot. His scalp prickled. The hair on his arms stood up. "I'm electrified," he cried. Then the food bag fell with a thud. Lightning stabbed the ridges.

Greg stumbled, enveloped in the billowing tarp. Ken ran to help, grabbing one end of the plastic sheet. Finally they managed to rope it up like a tent between the two trees, They set rocks to hold down the flapping sides.

"Look!" Greg pointed at a ridge. "It's on fire."

"Static electricity," yelled Ken. "Don't stand there staring, man." He threw the food bag into the shelter.

They ran around grabbing packs, pans, sleeping bags, mats—tossing everything under the tarp. They found more rocks to hold down the sides. The air smelled like rotten eggs; the ridge crackled as if alive.

"Lightning's gonna fry us," shrieked Greg.

"Get away from the trees."

"Why?"

As if in answer, a white bolt split a nearby lodgepole.

Greg beat on Ken's shoulder and pointed to the top of the granite slabs. "Caveman."

"He's beckoning," said Ken. "Come on."

"No."

"Okay, stay here. Get soaked." Ken clambered up the granite slabs. He glanced back, relieved to see Greg following.

When they'd climbed halfway to the cave, the wind stopped. An ominous stillness settled over the lake, slate gray clouds poised on the ridges. The sky darkened. A sudden blast of wind and a crack of lightning. Thunder roared. Then a waterfall poured from the sky.

Ken and Greg scrambled across the flat rock to the crevasse. Carefully they maneuvered down the wet, slippery footholds and across the ledge. They ducked into the cave, black as night, where a tiny fire sputtered.

Caveman built up the fire and set a pot of water on the flames. He hung his dripping shirt over the corner root and put on his khaki one. From a can he drew out a handful of dried leaves, crushing them into a tin cup.

As a fragrant odor wafted from the cup, Greg whispered in Ken's ear, "What's that stuff?"

"Mountain pennyroyal," Ken whispered back, recognizing the smell of wild mint. Old Domino often made him a cup from the leaves that grew near the horse corral.

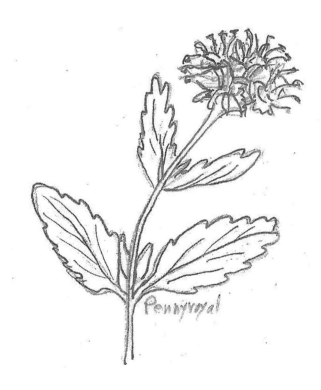

Pennyroyal

Caveman poured boiling water into the cup and stirred it with a spoon. He handed the drink to Ken who slurped a few pungent mouthfuls before passing it on. Greg took two sips, then returned the cup to its owner.

For nearly an hour the wind roared through treetops, lightning crackled, thunder boomed, and rain splashed on the outside ledge like waves over a ship's bow. Inside the cave, boys gulped mint tea in rotation and tried to dry their clothes near the fire. Occasionally they glanced sideways at each other, but so enveloped were they in the storm's violent sounds and flashes of light that they didn't talk.

When at last the rain stopped and the thunder rumbled away, Caveman crawled to the mouth of the cave. Ken joined him, breathed in the fresh air with deep gulps. The clouds had parted, revealing a sky so blue it looked scrubbed clean. Sunlight shafted through trees. The beams widened until the eastern side of the lake was bathed in light. Steam rose from the granite; rivulets raced toward the lake; a flock of finches chirped and flitted among the fir branches; from below, a frog croaked.

At last Ken found the courage to speak. "Thanks for your help."

Caveman nodded.

"What's your name?"

"Why do you wanna know?"

"Just would. Course, if you'd rather we just call you Caveman, then—"

"It's Matt," he said, moving back from the cave entrance. "You can leave now." His tone was an obvious dismissal.

Greg emerged from the cave like a bear out of hibernation. He squinted at Matt. "Thanks, but you ought to get rid of those ants." He squeezed past Ken and disappeared up the crevasse.

Ken listened to Greg's clunky climbing. He glanced back in the cave at Matt, who sat with his knees clasped to his chest. "Want to come for spaghetti tonight?"

"No. Got all I need here."

"Just trying to pay you back,"

"Forget it."

Ken shrugged. "You really want to live here all winter?"

Matt crawled forward and glared. "Told you so."

"Snowstorms are heavy, man, especially this high."

"I've camped before—lots of times. I know what I'm doing."

"In winter? On top of the Sierras?"

Matt crawled out on the ledge. Sunlight splotched yellow into his hair. He didn't answer.

For a moment Ken thought Matt's face held the look of a trapped animal. "Anyone else know you're here?"

"No. I hitched a ride to the Summit." Matt's eyes narrowed, and his voice turned hard. "Look, kid, you and your friend better not tell anybody about me."

"Why not?"

"Just don't."

Ken swallowed—a lump forming—the one that stuck in his throat whenever he faced a problem he wasn't sure how to solve. "Okay, if that's the way you want it."

"That's how I want it."

"Good luck then." Ken started up the crevasse. He paused, studied his wet boots, and tried to think of something else to say. He looked back at the cave. The entrance was empty.

CHAPTER 7—HOME

They woke up before dawn, the eastern sky faintly graying. Mist hovered on the lake, and the air felt like ice. Ken built a fire and blew on his fingers for warmth. Then he set a pan of water on the grill and fed a stick of wood into the flames. The only thing bad about this kind of morning was how it made his nose run. He sniffed and rubbed it with the back of his hand. Spreading his arms, he said to Greg, "This is the waiting hour."

"Whatever," said Greg, continuing to cram his sleeping bag into its stuff sack.

Ken said, "One time I woke up at five, looked out the loft window, and there on the edge of the forest was a mule deer. It raised its nose to the wind. Listened. Looked around. Waited to make sure there was no danger.

That's the way with birds, too. See that finch up there on the limb, feathers fluffed? It's waiting for the sun. Snakes, frogs, marmots—they don't jump into the day. I tell you, all the animals are waiting."

"Yeah, okay. Well, I'm loaded up, ready to go." Greg sat down by the fire and polished the blade of his pocketknife with the corner of his flannel shirt.

Ken sprinkled salt into the water and made another attempt to communicate his dawn theory. "Bet Matt's waiting for something. What do you think he's waiting for?"

"Who cares?"

"Don't you envy him?"

"What're you talking about?"

"Nobody tells him what to do. His father doesn't make fun of him or give lectures on what he's done wrong. He doesn't have to share anything with a wise-ass brother or—"

Greg snapped the blade shut and returned the knife to his pocket. "I'd hate to live alone."

Ken shot a look at Greg. "Yeah," he said, wishing he hadn't talked so much. He poured boiling water over the instant cereal. "Grab a spoon and dig in. Joe says, 'Gummy oatmeal sticks to ribs.'"

"Looks like glue all right."

Their climb to the crest wasn't as bad as Ken had anticipated. And the hike back seemed easy. Bees weren't yet in full flight, and knowing the trail made the way seem quicker. At the glen, while Greg took a leak behind a bush, Ken picked an elephant head for Carolyn, pressing the flower inside his topo map.

Five hours after leaving camp, they reached the trailhead. Only one car and a truck were parked there in the rest area. A lady was walking her dog, and two men were smoking cigarettes near a picnic table.

Ken dug into the pockets of his jeans. "Holy cripes! Got any change?" he asked Greg.

"No. Why do we need money?"

"For the pay phone, bonehead. To call Joe."

Greg squeezed up his face. "Nuts! Forgot to put money on the checklist."

"Yeah, you forgot about that." Ken didn't mention he'd lost the list. "Oh, man, what'll we do?"

"Bum money from one of these tourists. Or ask them for a ride."

"You do it," said Ken.

"I don't talk to strangers."

Ken kicked a pine cone and tried to think. To hike all the way to Soda Springs was impossible. Might be midnight before they got home. Besides, he wasn't sure his muscles could make it. "We'll head for Boreal Lodge," he said. "It's right across the highway. My brother knows a ski patrol guy there—Bill—lives in a trailer, usually hangs out around the lodge."

They walked through the underpass and up to the big wooden building. On the deck sat tall, wiry Bill Kernsey—clipboard in his hand, boots beside his chair, and stocking feet propped on the railing. He was drinking coffee with another man.

"Heading into the back country?" Bill asked the boys.

"No, heading out," Ken replied in a nonchalant manner. "Is there a...a free phone anyplace around here?"

"Why? Got a problem?"

"Yeah, need a ride home." Ken shifted his weight and tried to look cool.

"I'll take you as soon as I finish my paper work. But you'll have to ride outside in my truck bed. Got a ton of stuff in the passenger seat. What about your buddy?"

Greg said. "Uncle's picking me up at Ken's place. So—" His voice squeaked and he cleared his throat. "So, if you could take me along, I'd appreciate it."

"I'll meet you in the parking lot in 15 minutes. It's the orange truck." Bill grabbed his boots and disappeared into the lodge.

As the boys headed for the parking lot, Ken said triumphantly, "Well, I solved the problem. I'm excited about riding up the pass on the bed of a truck. Aren't you?"

"Not particularly," said Greg, making a face. "Seems like we're just a couple of dumb dogs."

During the drive to the cabin neither boy spoke. Ken kept thinking how next time he'd make a list of everything needed, including money, and he wouldn't lose the list. His thought grew hazy near the Summit. So tired....

Greg's uncle, already in Soda Springs visiting friends, picked up his nephew before Ken staggered to the dinner table. Without the promise of a hot fudge sundae, he wouldn't have made it through the ham and sweet potatoes. He had trouble keeping his eyes open.

Ian leaned back in his chair. "How'd you manage with the storm?"

Ken yawned. "Stayed in a cave."

"You went into a cave during a storm?"

"Kenny," said Mr. Reede, setting his fork neatly on his plate, "you could get electrocuted by leaning on rock walls."

"Even standing beside them," added Ian.

Ken blinked and pushed his plate away. "Well, I didn't get electrocuted."

"The best thing to do," said Mr. Reede, "is squat on your toes and keep your head down, like this." He rose from the table and demonstrated.

"For an hour?" Ken inquired.

"In that case, you should kneel on insulated material like the rubber pad under your sleeping bag."

"Away from trees and high ground," Ian emphasized.

"Sure, sure." Ken wished they'd lay off. Why were they always after him?

"Did you see any other campers around?" Ian asked.

"Yeah, two kids and their dad at the mouth of Prosser Creek."

"That's all? Good. I plan to hike to the lake next week. Where's the cave?"

Ken straightened, suddenly awake. "Not really a cave. More of a ledge—a shelf sort of thing. Don't bother with it. Anyway, the lake looks polluted. I wouldn't go there."

"Polluted? That's hard to believe." Ian speared another slice of ham and smothered it with raison sauce. "In that case, think I'll head for the American River."

After that, Ken lost track of the conversation. In his mind he lay in his sleeping bag next to a campfire, surrounded by cliffs crowned with moonlight, staring at their reflection in a crystal-clear lake.

"Kenny," his mother said, "here's your sundae."

His eyes barely focused on the heaping dish. It smelled like something made in heaven, but he couldn't pick up his spoon. "Stick it in the freezer," he heard himself say.

He heaved himself up the loft ladder. Gypsy brushed against his legs and meowed until he scratched her ears. He took off his boots, dropping each one with a clump.

His mattress felt like feathers. He drifted away—marmots watching from rocks, thunder rumbling in the distance, a Clark's nutcracker flying beside him. For a while he lay enveloped in a meadow of flowers while bees droned overhead.

His last thought was of Carolyn. Tomorrow he'd give her the elephant-head flower....

CHAPTER 8—CLOUDS

Ken and Greg made three more camping trips that summer—two-day expeditions on weekends. "Can't take any more time," Greg explained to Ken over the phone. "Got this job. Helping Uncle Gus with deliveries in Truckee. He needs me."

"No problem," said Ken. "We're getting good at short treks. Don't forget stuff anymore."

"Right. Next summer I'll have a whole week free after school's out."

"Great. Let's plan a six-day backpack trip. How about tackling the mountains above Lake Tahoe. Get a bird's eye view of the lake."

"Sounds good to me."

One evening, Ken sprawled on the sheepskin rug next to Gypsy and stared out the window. Patches of evening sky darkened between lodgepole branches. It had been a good day except for having to sweep the pine needles off the front porch and clean the roof gutters—chores his father laid on him. "Why can't Ian do it?" he had asked.

"He's at Donner Lake, fishing for our supper," his father had said.

Ken had frowned. Ian was always doing something important for the family.

After his chores were finished, Ken had grabbed an apple out of the back porch cooler and hiked to the top of Soda Springs Ski Hill. As he sat under the twisted Jeffrey pine and ate, he surveyed Summit Valley.

This was his mountain-rimmed territory: Lake Van Norden to the east; Ice Lakes to the South; Interstate 80 to the west; and Soda Springs below with Carolyn's cabin in the middle. He started downhill. Time for a visit.

Since returning from Warren Lake, he'd visited Carolyn every afternoon except for the days he'd been camping with Greg. Often she would ask about the ski hill she saw through her window. "Tell me about the Jeffrey pine," she would say, "and the crutose lichens."

This afternoon they had looked through travel magazines and planned a safari to East Africa where they would gather plant specimens, photograph wild animals, and climb Mt. Kilimanjaro. Before he knew it, an hour had passed and Mrs. Jamison was saying, "Carolyn, you should rest now."

Then he'd spent some time with Joe, watching him make mushroom soup and lasagna. The broth simmering on a back burner had filled the air with a wet-earth smell. Gradually, rich odors of cheese, onions and tomatoes wafted from the oven. As if inspired, Joe sang an aria from "La Boheme. "

"It's about a guy named Rudolpho who meets a lovely lady named Mimi," Joe said.

When Ken told him about Carolyn, Joe smiled. "Women are the flowers of the human race."

At that moment, Velma burst through the swinging door. "That lasagna," she snarled, "when's it gonna be ready?"

"In twenty minutes," Joe yelled. "Why you got to know?"

"If someone comes for dinner, you numbskull, I need to tell them when they'll get it." She charged back though the door,

"You're a lousy thistle among the beautiful flowers," Joe had yelled after her.

And Ken had laughed all the way home.

Now that the day was over, he lay on the sheepskin rug in the loft, relaxing. With the trap door open, he could hear his mother and father talking in the living room. They didn't know he was home. He had sneaked up to the loft while they were in the kitchen. Figured if he kept out of sight his father couldn't corner him for another job. Ian wasn't back yet from Donner Lake, probably spending more time water-skiing than fishing. At least next week his nerdy brother would return to college. Then, once more, the loft would be Ken's private domain. He relished the peace and comfort of it. Not at all like Matt's cave.

What makes a guy hide out in a cave? Was he a high school dropout, a runaway from home? Were his parents hunting for him, wondering where he was? Of course, he could be older than he looked. Maybe he'd lost a job and was homeless. Or he might've committed a crime and the cops were after him. Could be a dope dealer or a murderer.

Surely nothing that bad.

"Carolyn...."

The word drifted up through the trap door opening. It sent a shiver through his body. Why were they talking about her? He crawled over closer to listen.

"So, Tom gave up his job," his father said. "Since Carolyn always wanted to live in the mountains, he decided this was something he could do for her."

"How tragic!" said his mother.

"There are treatments that could prolong her life."

Ken drew back from the opening, his heart pounding.

His father said, "They've made arrangements with Tahoe Forest Hospital."

"How long do they think she'll live?"

"You can't tell with this type of leukemia."

Ken softly closed the trap door and pressed his face on Gypsy's warm fur. Her purr was like a faraway storm.

With an effort he rose and picked up the topo map from his desk. He switched on his lamp and stared at the lakes on the map. He fingered the swirls of contour lines that he now knew indicated elevations, but his mind couldn't comprehend them. With a sigh, he folded up the map and turned off the light. He considered going to bed so he could get up early to follow the buck he'd heard this morning. The animal had stood near the porch, rubbing velvet off its horns against a tree. If he went to bed now, he could get up early and find that buck and see how clean his horns were. But it was almost time for dinner. He couldn't miss a meal. They wouldn't understand. He wouldn't be able to explain. Besides, how could he sleep?

For a while he sat at his desk, trying to think about the deer, trying to plan a hike over Phipps Pass, trying to think about school, about Joe, Greg, Old Domino, Matt—about anything other than Carolyn. He lay down on the sheepskin rug and stared out the window, barely able to make out shapes of branches.

Footsteps clumped across the front porch and Ian's voice hailed his arrival with two big fish. With a supreme effort, Ken opened the trap door and yelled down, "Hey, Mom, when's dinner?"

"Didn't know you were home," his father called up. "About ready to go looking for you."

"Well, I'm here."

"Supper's in half an hour," his mother announced.

It took three days for Ken to gather enough courage to visit Carolyn.

"I've missed you," she said. "Where've you been? Here, have a plum." She pointed to the bowl of fruit on the table.

He grabbed a plum and bit into it.

She propped her elbows on the table and stared out the window. "It's starting to look like fall. Aspens turning color. Did you know gooseberries grow in back of our cabin?"

"No," he said huskily, "but I thought they might."

"Yeah, they do." She gestured at the window. "Are there gooseberries up there?"

"On top of the ski hill? No."

She leaned back in her chair and giggled. "You've got plum juice on your nose."

"Hm-m, well, I got a bandanna here someplace." He yanked out a wad of gum wrappers. "Holy cripes, I left it home."

She giggled again and handed him a paper napkin.

"Thanks." He had a hard time meeting her eyes. "Where were we?"

"On top of the ski hill."

"Oh, yeah. Wild onions grow up there. Old Domino uses them in stews."

"Sounds good. When I'm well, I'll get some. We'll climb up there together."

"Okay." He swallowed hard and crumpled up the napkin.

"We'll sit in the red chairlift and look at the valley. I'll inspect the twisted Jeffrey pine and check out the volcanic rocks with the lichens. We'll pick a bunch of wild onions and bring them home. I'll cook you a special stew."

"Sure," he managed to say, "that's just what we'll do." He swallowed hard and stood up. "Well, got to go now. See you tomorrow."

In early September, the Basque herded his sheep into Summit Valley. He camped for a night in the meadow near Lake Van Norden. Ken was on the front porch when he heard the sheep bleating, bells tinkling and a dog barking. He saw the sheep across the road, followed by the dog—a black and white ball of energy that kept the flock headed in the right direction.

Ken hurried over to meet the Basque, a short man with massive shoulders, shaggy hair and eyes as blue as a summer sky.

"I still have the sheepskin rug you gave me," Ken told him.

"Thought so," the Basque replied.

"How come you're heading down the mountains so early?"

"Winter coming."

"We haven't finished fall yet."

"Winter coming," the Basque repeated. "I see signs. Snow soon, you know. It come soon."

Ken studied the dark clouds barreling up in the afternoon and thought about Matt in the cave.

Fall was taking over the mountains Aspens had burst into golden yellow. Leaves quivered in the wind with the sound of far-off waves. Gooseberries reddened.

At the end of each school day, after the Truckee bus dropped him off at Soda Springs Lodge, Ken visited Carolyn. On his way home, he followed the railroad tracks until he could see the lake. There he would stand, a foot on each rail, and stare at the water, the meadow, the forest, the clouds, the mountains.

The lake looked more and more foreboding. Along the shore, dark gray, water-marked boulders and snags became monsters. His fishing rocks turned into gravestones. At the eastern end of the lake, dry grass whispered secrets. Wind gusted, whisking off leaves, sweeping willows skeleton-clean. Masses of clouds churned up and raced across the sky as if sending a message. And every day as he stared at the mountains to the north, their peaks shrouded in mist, he thought about Matt.

CHAPTER 9—DECISION

On a cold Saturday afternoon in late September, when the sun threw long shadows, Ken sneaked over to the railroad sheds beyond Sugar Bowl Ski Area and secretly watched the switchmen cut a boxcar from a train. Pretending to be a spy, he slithered behind rocks and flattened against walls. He crawled through ditches on his stomach. Although he knew it was kid stuff, that didn't stop him.

Time to meet Secret Agent number four.

He plunged through a field of long-leafed mule ears that rustled with a ghostly sound. By the time he reached the safety zone at the west end of the lake, his fantasy faded. He found himself wondering if Matt had enough food and if Carolyn knew what her sickness was.

Last night he hadn't slept well. In his dreams he'd tried to scale a cliff but couldn't reach the top. Twice Matt was on the ridge—other times, Carolyn—once, nobody—only the reflection of a hidden moon. He woke up in a cold sweat, clutching the covers so hard his hands hurt.

Now, remembering his dream, he hurled pebbles at the metal sign identifying the Yuba River, feeling a satisfaction with each ping. But soon that grew tiresome. He walked across the small bridge and along the south side of the river that fed into the lake. The water level in the river was low, barely a stream. Feeling everything was caught on hold, he sank down on the river bank.

A tiny meadow mouse crept out of a tunnel in the dirt and pivoted its head. Seeing Ken, the mouse backed up to the hole and scooted inside. Ken peered into the tunnel. Light reflecting off the eyes of the mouse made them look like ball bearings. Up and down they moved with the creature's frightened breathing.

"I'm not your enemy," Ken whispered. Again he thought about Matt—about what the Basque had said: "Snow soon, you know. Tomorrow I truck my sheep to the lowlands."

Zipping up his jacket, he saw that the sleeves were too short. He leaned back on the bank and studied the clouds. The same kind had developed every afternoon for a week. Not storm clouds. By night they'd be gone. Yet the air felt unusually cold for this early in fall. Old Domino would know if winter would come early.

The old man was loading saddles into his truck when Ken swung over the corral fence. "Hey, man," Ken called to him, "need help?"

Domino scratched his scraggly beard, the lines on his ruddy face crinkling deeper. "Yep. Bring the saddle blankets outta there." He nodded toward the storeroom near his one-room cabin.

Ken brought him the pile of blankets. "You moving back to Auburn?"

"Yep!" Domino tossed the blankets onto the truck bed and threw a bunch of halters on top of them.

"Aren't you heading down earlier than usual?"

Domino nodded.

"How come?"

"Winter's gettin' ready to drop."

"How can you tell?"

"Animal signs. Here, help me with this grain sack."

"Okay."

In the low rays of the sun, Domino's wrinkled face looked like bark. "Hold 'er there," he cried and climbed into the truck bed. "Now, push. Good." He jumped to the ground. "That's it."

Ken said, "Guess I won't be seeing you for a while?"

"Guess not." Domino squinted. "Want some chicken soup?"

"Sure."

Ken followed him into the one-room cabin and closed the door. On top of the pot-bellied stove bubbled a pan of soup that smelled wonderful, like the kind his mother made when a blizzard came.

The old man tossed his weathered cowboy hat on the bunk and hung his denim jacket on a wall hook. He took Ken's jacket and hung it over his. Shoving a wooden box close to the stove, he said, "Have a seat."

"Thanks."

Domino stirred the soup.

Ken said, "How do animals let you know about winter?"

Domino took two mugs off the shelf under the window, lifted a ladle from a wall nail, dipped it into the soup and filled the cups. "Grab that tin of crackers on the shelf behind you and stick it here on the floor 'tween us." He handed Ken a mug. "Only got one spoon, but I prefer slurpin' noodles."

"Me too," said Ken."Don't need a spoon."

Domino sat on the other box, edging it close to the fire.

After a slurp which burned his tongue, Ken said, "Tell me about those animal signs."

"All right. It's gonna be an early winter 'cause deer've already moved lower." Domino blew on his soup. "Another sign: birds leavin' early, 'cept ones that stay up here all winter. Also, yellow jackets nestin' deeper. Chipmunks and squirrels runnin' faster. Mice gettin' into everything. Animals have better knowin' than us. Once we had the knowin' till we got civilized."

With one hand, he gingerly opened the stove door and tossed in a hunk of wood. A puff of smoke brought out the smell of burning pine. He kicked the door shut with a bang. "I like to think I'm goin' backwards from civilization."

"How long you been going backwards?"

"'Bout 35 years. I reckon if I keep lookin' and listenin' another 35, I'll know how nature works. Course by then I'd be 109. Might not be around." He slurped. "Yep, winter's in the air."

Ken slurped. "Domino, if a guy was to live in a mountain cave—what are his chances of surviving winter?"

The old man's eyes narrowed until they were nearly hidden. "All depends on the elevation."

"Let's say 8200 feet."

"If he's got a good ax and a better than good saw, and if he starts workin' in July, he might have enough wood to last it. But up that high there ain't a lot of trees. And he'd have to know which stuff burns too fast and which is so green it hardly burns. And he'd have to have a big dry area to store his wood."

Ken took too big a slurp. His lips tingled, and his throat burned. Ignoring his discomfort, he plunged on. "The guy might not have the tools either."

Old Domino said, "Nobody could survive in a cave without a good set of tools."

"And he might think he could pick up old pieces of wood from the ground the way he did in the summer."

"He'd have to be an awful good mountain man to last a winter that high. Course, in an emergency, he could pull off dead, lower limbs on lodgepoles, but they wouldn't last long.
'Sides, he's gotta have a cave full of food. Hope you ain't thinkin' of doin' it."

"No, I wouldn't do anything so dumb."

"Good, cause after a couple of blizzards, snow can get so deep a fella wouldn't be able to get out. Yep, he'd be isolated, frozen stiff like a side of beef in a food locker till he thawed out in spring and rotted away. Course, wolves and coyotes and vultures would eat him up long before that. Want more soup?"

"No thanks." Ken swallowed hard and handed him the mug. "Tasted good, though."

Domino's laugh sounded like water sputtering against a stove.

Ken noticed the sun was almost down. "I better get going." He pulled on his jacket and yanked up the zipper. "So long. See you next spring."

"'Spect so." The old man's face cracked into a warm smile. He followed Ken to the door.

Ken bolted over the fence. He took a last look at Old Domino, standing in the cabin doorway, squinting at the sky. He waved and then dashed for the road.

When he reached the bridge, a Steller's jay shattered the air with warning squawks. A golden-mantled ground squirrel chirred from a stump then disappeared. A red-tailed hawk circled overhead—silent, dark against the bright sky as it dipped, searching for movement below.

A mouse scurried across the meadow followed by the shadow of the raptor. The hawk's dive was straight and swift.

Ken heard a squeal. He couldn't look. He ran faster. The growl of an engine and clack of wheels on a track intruded until they filled the air. A train chugged up the steep grade from the east. Ken chanted to the sounds: "Got to go back to Warren Lake, got to go back to Warren Lake...."

The train was only a few miles away, but Ken didn't put an ear to the humming rails as he usually did. That seemed silly in light of his momentous decision.

CHAPTER 10—SECRETS

Ken sat down in his usual chair across from Carolyn. "You aren't a blabbermouth are you?" he said.

It was Friday afternoon. Ken and Greg had just gotten off the school bus at Soda Springs Lodge. Greg was still at the foot of the path, having discovered a long-horned beetle in the pine needles. An excuse, Ken realized, to let him visit Carolyn alone. Good old Greg.

"Course I'm not a blabbermouth," Carolyn replied. "What's there to blabber about anyway?"

"Greg and I are hiking back to Warren Lake."

"When?"

"Sh-h-h! Tomorrow."

She lowered her voice. "How come I'm supposed to be quiet?"

"Cause nobody's supposed to know."

"How come?"

"If they knew, we couldn't make the trip."

"I don't get it."

Ken glanced around to make certain her mother and father hadn't come into the room. "Well, it's not a good time of year to go. If my folks knew, they'd stop us."

"Then don't go."

"We have to."

"Why?"

"To save somebody."

"Who?"

"A guy. Can't tell you anything about him."

"Why not?"

"I made a promise not to. Now, listen. This is what you should know." He leaned forward. She leaned closer. He noticed how tired she looked, and sadness rushed though him. Her cheeks were so pale he wanted to rub warmth into them. But he was afraid to touch her, as if she might break.

"Early tomorrow morning," he whispered, "Joe's driving us to Boreal Ridge Lodge—across the highway from the trailhead. Joe thinks we're spending the night near the lodge in Bill's trailer."

"Who's Bill?"

"The guy who heads the ski-patrol up there."

"But if you take your packs along, won't Joe be suspicious?"

"That's why we plan to seal them inside a huge cardboard box. I found the box yesterday behind the ski shop."

Carolyn wrinkled her nose. "You'll have to tell Joe what's in the box."

"We're saying it's ski equipment. We're delivering it to Bill 'cause the shop doesn't have a truck on the Summit yet."

"And he believed you?"

"Joe doesn't pry into people's business."

"What're you telling your parents?"

"That we're spending Saturday night in Bill's trailer, that he's got ski movies for us to see. I didn't think my father would go for the delivery idea. He'd want to look inside the box, count everything, make an inventory. I've hidden the box from him. Hidden it from my mom, too, or she'd tell my father about it for sure. I hate being sneaky like this, but I didn't know how else to do it."

"What are you saving this guy from?"

"Winter. If he stays up there he might...die."

"Oh." She looked down at her hands.

He wet his lips. "We hike into Warren Lake tomorrow, stay overnight, and start home Sunday morning. The minute we get back to the trailhead, I'll call you." Again he wet his lips. "If I don't call you by 4:00, phone my folks and tell them where we went."

"You're thinking something awful could happen to you."

"Course not."

"If it weren't dangerous, you'd tell your parents. You're telling me 'cause you need someone to know where you've gone."

"Well, yeah, sure, there's a little risk. Nothing to worry about. Just you work on feeling healthy."

"I do. Every day I tell myself, *I'm going to get well, I'm going to get well.* I look out this window and that's what I say."

She rubbed her cheeks hard and stared through the window. "I'd give anything to be able to climb that ski hill. Probably because I see it every day. I look out and keep imagining what it would be like to sit under that old Jeffrey Pine up there. Then I could look out over the whole valley, couldn't I? "

"Yeah, you could see it all. Someday we'll go up there together."

She nodded. "We'll go together." Her face turned serious. "Ken, please be careful. If something happened to you, I...I couldn't bear it."

"I'll be careful," he said quickly, not daring to look at her again. "Look, I'll call you Sunday afternoon." The words scarcely came out. Somehow he made it to the front door.

"Hey," Greg yelled as Ken swept past him, "where're you going?"

"Oh, hi. Forgot you were out here."

"Is something wrong?"

"No."

"Seeing Carolyn makes you goofy."

"What're you talking about? You're nuts."

Greg heaved the duffel bag on his head, attempting to balance it. "You're right. Watching that long-horned beetle must've affected my mind."

"Yeah," said Ken, "guess your long-horned beetle affected me too."

They both burst into laughter, staggering around, the duffle bag falling down between them.

CHAPTER 11—CATASTROPHE

Even though the trap door was closed, Ken and Greg huddled on the sheepskin rug and spoke in hushed tones as if Mrs. Reede, below in the kitchen, might have superhuman hearing.

"Let's wear two pairs of socks," Ken whispered, "cotton under, wool over—warmer that way. And I'm taking my wool shirt. I'll wear it under my parka."

"Me too. What about my empty duffel?"

"Give it here." Ken shoved the duffel under his bed. He pointed to a bulging shopping bag on his desk. "See that? It's full of newspapers, but we'll say it's our overnight clothes for Boreal. Got to make it look like that's where we're really going."

"Right!" Greg revealed a small metal box. "Tinder," he mouthed and slid open the top to reveal wood shavings and pine needles. "This dry stuff will help us start a fire even in the rain."

"Good thinking. Don't forget the matches."

"Right! Got'em." Greg closed the lid. It snapped shut with a pop, startling them both.

Downstairs, a door opened and footsteps moved across the back porch, followed by a clunk, a rustle and another clunk.

Greg froze. "What's that?"

"My mother, getting something from the freezer for dinner."

More footsteps, then a door closing.

Ken crawled across the room, Greg following. "Here's Ian's backpack."

"What if your brother comes home this weekend?"

"He didn't say he would. Anyway, he wouldn't be looking for his pack this time of year."

They crawled back to Ken's side of the room, Greg clutching the pack to his chest.

"Did you remember to take money for a phone call?" Greg asked.

Ken nodded. He reached into his desk drawer. "And I've got two little mirrors. Good for signaling with the sun. You know, in case we get separated.

"Better not get separated."

"Well, you never know what might happen. Okay, let's bring the big box up here so we can load in our packs and tape it shut."

"Now?"

"Yeah, before my father gets home. While I keep Mom occupied in the kitchen, you get it from under the porch and drag it up into the loft. When you're done, give an all-clear signal."

"Like what?"

"A coyote yip?"

Greg made a face. "I don't know why I let you talk me into this. If Caveman ends up in a glacier, that's his business. I don't like making up phony stories and sneaking around like a criminal. And I can't yip like a coyote."

"Sure you can. Look, if you don't want to do this, you don't have to. I'll hike in by myself."

"Then I'd feel even worse. Come on, let's get the box."

Quietly, Ken opened the trap door and crept down the ladder. Greg followed.

Ken ambled through the kitchen doorway and pulled the door shut behind him. In a dramatic manner, he sniffed the aroma rising from the iron pot on the stove. "What a great smell, Mom. I can't think of a better smell, except when you bake a chocolate cake or cook applesauce."

Then came scratching sounds from the living room. Ken's voice rose an octave. "Can we have hot garlic bread with whatever you're making in the pot? And a big salad and the rest of that spice cake? Or did we finish the spice cake? I can't remember."

"Kenny, why are you yelling like that? I told you at breakfast that I planned to make lamb stew. As for the spice cake, you ate the rest of it before you went to bed last night."

"Oh, yeah. I forgot about that."

Mrs. Reede continued, "We're having butterscotch pudding because your father likes it." She frowned. "Sounds like Greg's fiddling with the loft ladder. Go see what he's doing. I don't want him scratching up the floor."

Ken flipped on the counter radio and tuned into a country music station.

"Turn that down," his mother cried. "What's gotten into you this afternoon?"

"Butterscotch pudding," Ken yelled. "Fantastic! Wow, butterscotch pudding."

"Since when have you liked butterscotch pudding? You usually make one of your faces when we have it. Now, go find out what's making that scraping noise."

Ken backed toward the living room door. "Yeah, sure, I'll take care of that."

The kitchen door shot open and banged into him.

"Watch it," he snapped as Greg peered around the door frame.

"Say, Ken," said Greg. "Can I talk to you a minute?"

The two retreated from the kitchen.

"Box is too big," Greg whispered. "Can't squeeze it through the loft opening. See, it's stuck."

Ken groaned. "You can't leave it dangling up there. Take it back outside. Hide it where you found it. And hurry up. My father's due any minute. We'll wait till the middle of the night. Then, we'll take our packs down and box them up under the porch."

Ken returned to the kitchen. "Everything's okay, Mom. I think Stubby's trying to burrow into the house."

Mrs. Reede started for the living room door.

"No, Mom." Ken jumped in front of her. "Just kidding. It isn't Stubby. It's Greg. He's—ah—practicing tricks."

"On the ladder?"

"No, wait, wait. He gets embarrassed when people watch him. Self-conscious, you know, the way I am sometimes. Like when I go fishing and Ian hogs the worms."

By the time Mrs. Reede made it through the doorway, the living room was empty.

"Where 's Greg performing?" she inquired, hands on her hips.

"Guess he quit for the day."

Mr. Reede's voice burst out from the front path, "Greg, why are you staggering across the porch with that huge box? Look out for the steps."

Ken heard a wild yell and two thuds, followed by a moment of silence. Mrs. Reede rushed to the screen door.

Ken collapsed on the couch and closed his eyes. He heard the screen door open and Greg limp inside. He heard his father clear his throat in an authoritative way.

"I fell on top of the box," Greg announced. "It's smashed."

Ken's eyes flew open. He glared at Greg. "Did you break your ankle?"

"No, but it hurts."

"That's a relief—I mean, it's a relief your ankle's not broken."

Mrs. Reede asked, "What's the trick, Greg?"

"Trick?"

Ken said quickly, "I told Mom you were working on balancing tricks. Don't you sometimes use three boxes?"

"Oh, yeah, right," said Greg. "I'm not very good with three boxes."

Mr. Reede said, "You don't appear good with one."

"Kenny," Mrs. Reede said, "help Greg into the kitchen. Jim, get an ice pack from the freezer and an ace bandage from the bathroom. It's in the bottom drawer."

Mr. Reede quickly retrieved both items and set them on the kitchen table. "Greg, do you realize you could've killed yourself."

"I'm fine," insisted Greg. "My foot needs a night of rest, that's all. I'm fine, I tell you."

"I hope so," Ken said between clenched teeth. "Man, why'd you fall down the steps?"

Greg sank into a kitchen chair and unlaced his right boot. "I did it on purpose," he growled, "to bug you."

"You wanted to get out of the trip." Ken glanced at his father. "The trip to Boreal Ridge, that is."

"Blah, blah, blah!" Greg yelled at him and threw his boot under the table.

"Stop squabbling," Mr. Reede barked. "Act like adults for a change."

"Gracious," said Mrs. Reede, "the windows are clouding up."

"That's the steam from your stew," proclaimed Mr. Reede.

"Oh, is it now?" Mrs. Reede's eyes sparkled mischievously. "I thought it was from all the hot air blowing around here."

Nobody spoke for a long time after that.

As Mrs. Reede tended to Greg's ankle, late afternoon sunlight shone through the kitchen window and glinted on her granite-colored hair.

CHAPTER 12—LOADING

"You awake?" Greg called softly from Ian's bed.

"Yeah," Ken said. "How's your ankle?"

"Could be worse. What time is it?"

"A little after midnight."

"Shall we take the packs down now?"

"Okay, but I'll do it. Don't want you falling any more."

Ken switched on the flashlight and crept out from under the covers. Gypsy, curled up on the desk, opened an eye and watched him pull on a navy sweatshirt and warm-up pants. He slipped his feet into a pair of moccasins.

Greg winced as he tried to stand on his ankle. "It'll be okay by morning," he said.

"Better be." Ken picked up the roll of tape beside Gypsy. He opened the trap door and listened. "They're asleep," he whispered. "My father's snoring; mom's making snuffling sounds. Now listen, man, after I go down the ladder, hand me the packs." Ken gave Greg the flashlight. "Shine this below. That'll let me see enough to raid the kitchen. Then, I'll lug the packs outside, stuff them into the box and tape the cardboard together. When I'm done, I'll drag the box down and hide it in the bushes by the road."

He jammed the roll of tape into his sweatshirt pocket. "After I go outside, you switch off the light and watch from the front window till I come back on the porch. Then shine the light down on the loft ladder so I can find it. If you hear noise from my parents' bedroom, turn off the light and close the trap door. I'll hide until it's quiet again. Can't let them discover me. Mom's already suspicious."

"How'll you see when you get outside?"

"The stars'll give me enough light."

"You've got things pretty well figured out," Greg said.

"Hope so." Ken started down the ladder.

Everything was working according to Ken's plan. He sneaked the food and packs out of the house and under the porch, loaded them into the box, taped it shut and dragged it down the path. The night was cold and clear. Every sound magnified. He worried that his dragging was too noisy. Every few feet he stopped to listen for sounds from the cabin.

Nothing.

He hid the box in the bushes, hurried back on the path, up the steps and across the porch.

Just as he reached the front door, he heard Gypsy screech.

The trap door banged shut. A lamp in the living room flashed on. Ken flattened against the side of the house.

From the living room, Mr. Reede shouted, "Kenny, what's happening up there?"

After a moment, Greg called down, "Sorry, Mr. Reede. When I got out of bed to try my ankle, I stepped on the cat's tail."

What happened next chilled Ken more than the night air. His father shot the bolt across the front door. Now he was locked out of the house.

Eventually the living room light went out. Ken peered through the porch window. A lamp was switched on in his parents' bedroom, their door left open. His father sat up in bed, eating from a large container. Finishing the butterscotch pudding, eating from the main bowl—something he told Ken never to do.

Ken fought back a sense of indignation. An owl hooted from the branches of a lodgepole. Then, silence. Leaning against the house, he tried to think of an alternative to sleeping under the porch, but concluded no place outside was warm enough.

A whisper broke the stillness. "Ken, you out there?"

Greg's head was in the loft window.

"My father's locked me out," Ken whispered back.

"I'll sneak down and unlock the door."

"No, he'll see you. He's sitting in bed eating all the pudding."

"Then I'll sneak down after he goes back to sleep."

"I can't wait. Too cold. Besides, you'd probably fall. Is Gypsy okay?"

"Think so. She's under your bed."

"Good." Ken eyed the height to the loft window. "Hang the food bag rope out the window. I'll shinny up."

"Can't. It's in your pack."

"Holy cripes!" Ken pursed his lips and shivered. "Okay, so here's what you do. Roll up my bedspread lengthwise. Tight as you can. Hang it out the window."

"Don't think I can hold your weight."

"There's a piece of rope in my desk drawer. Use it to tie the bedspread to the chair. Then, set the chair under the window and straddle it. Chair can't go through the window."

"Right!"

On the first attempt, the end of the bedspread ripped. On the second try, Greg tied the rope further down and held onto bunched edges for further support, but Ken's hands kept sliding off. Finally, after a running jump and a fierce set of clutchings, Ken clambered up the bedspread, crawled through the window and fell onto Greg, nearly tipping over the chair. "Sh-h-h," they both said, untangling themselves.

Shivering, Ken jumped under his blankets and scrunched up into a ball. "Greg," he whispered, "take the flashlight to bed with you. Don't want you tripping on my rug."

Greg pulled the bedspread back though the window. "I won't trip. While you stood on the porch figuring what to do, I shoved the rug under your bed. Gypsy's sleeping on it."

"Good thinking, man

CHAPTER 13—RETURN

"Drop us here in the parking lot," Ken said to Joe as they drove into Boreal. "Don't bother to stay. Bill's going to help us carry the box to the lodge."

Ken felt guilty about the lies. They seemed to multiply. When this operation was over, he'd apologize to everybody. Even so, his folks might never believe him again. Joe might tell him to stay away. Ken, the liar—that's what they'd call him.

On the other hand, he'd promised Matt not to tell where he was. He couldn't renege on a promise. Wasn't it more important to save someone's life, even if you had to tell a few lies? Except the lies were getting bigger.

"Thanks for the ride," he said to Joe as he and Greg lifted the box out of the truck bed.

"Bet your life," Joe replied. "Any time I'm free, I take you where you need to go. That box looks pretty beat up. Hope the ski gear isn't damaged."

"No, it's all soft stuff. You know, parkas, ski pants...."

Early morning rays filtered through the trees and sparkled on the frosty roof of Boreal Lodge. Joe drove away, singing a sad, beautiful aria. In the cold, crystal air, his full tenor echoed through the empty parking lot and then faded into the rumble of trucks climbing the highway to the summit.

The boys tore open the box and pulled out their packs. Quickly they put them on, adjusting straps and belts. After stamping the cardboard box flat, they tossed it along with the shopping bag full of newspapers into the lodge dumpster.

Ken headed for the underpass. His breath sent out small puffs. Forest shadows reached out. The icy surface of the ground crunched under foot.

"Wait up," Greg called. "Go slow so my ankle adjusts."

Across the highway, the rest area was deserted. A clutter of plastic cups and fast-food wrappers lay under one of the picnic tables.

"Disgusting," said Greg. "Bet the trail will look ugly, too."

"We aren't here for scenery," Ken shot back and hurried toward the trailhead.

By mid-morning Greg had lagged far behind. Ken leaned against a boulder and waited for him to catch up. "You're limping."

"I've got a small problem." Greg sat on a log and loosened the lace on his right boot.

"Last time you stopped, it was to fix a twisted strap on your pack. Time before that, you had to look at the map. I think those are excuses to get the weight off your ankle. It's hurting a lot, isn't it?"

"No problem. I'm ready to go on now."

In less than an hour, Greg suggested they stop to eat.

"It's only 11:00," Ken said.

"Well, I'm hungry."

Sitting in a dry streambed, they divided a tin of corned beef, broke off hunks of garlic bread, and drank orange juice from their water bottles. Ken figured they had plenty of food left: apples, cheese, noodles, two cans of Spam, dried milk, four packages of instant oatmeal, sugar, jerky and a bag of hard candy. He displayed his checklist and felt pleased with his efficiency..

"How's the ankle?" Ken asked Greg after lunch.

"Fine."

"I don't think so."

Greg looked away. "Then, why'd you ask?"

"I'm wondering about you hiking down to the lake."

"I'll make it."

"You know how steep that is."

"I'll make it. I'll make it."

"Look, man, I'm not going to think you're chicken. Level with me. How's your ankle?"

Greg swallowed hard. "It's killing me."

Ken chewed on the edge of his lower lip and looked across the bowl to the ridge where the trail started down to the lake. He calculated the time it took when they hiked it before and how much longer it would take to get there now.

"Can you make it to the saddle?" Ken asked.

Greg nodded.

"Okay. Let's do this. You camp on the ridge. I'll hike down, stay overnight and come back with Matt in the morning."

"What if he won't come out with you?"

"If he refuses, I'll tell him we won't keep his secret, that when we get back to Boreal, we'll tell everybody where his cave is." Ken stowed his water bottle and stood up. "We'll flash signals to each other—sun on our mirrors. That way you'll know where I am."

"Don't like being separated," said Greg. "It's a wilderness rule to stay together."

"I know. But if you get down there and can't climb out, we're screwed."

Greg sighed. "Yeah. Right! Okay, I'll camp on the ridge."

They continued the hike, crossing the bee meadow, now dry and brown. Two more rest stops for Greg before they reached the saddle. Once there, Greg threw off his pack and collapsed to the ground, his face covered in sweat. With shaky fingers, he undid the lacing and gently eased off the boot, his face contorted with pain.

Ken noticed swollen flesh above the ankle. "Better loosen the bandage. Looks too tight."

While Greg rewrapped his ankle, Ken checked over the food supply, making sure it was divided evenly. "I'll send you a signal from the lake at

2:30," he said. "Again at 3:30 from the cave. Take care of yourself." He clapped Greg on the shoulder. "See you in the morning."

He started down the trail, trying to keep calm. No sense worrying.

At the level area before the final dip, he squinted up at the saddle. Too far to see Greg. But what he saw made his heart beat faster. Huge clouds barreled in from the southwest. Caution gone, Ken spurted down the trail. Talus gave way. He slid. Caught himself on a tree root. On he plunged. Finally he reached the lake and sank onto a log, panting, staring at the sky. Clouds boiled across. Not a leaf moved on the trees. He knew what was happening. The Basque's voice pounded in his ears, "Snow soon...snow soon...snow soon....

CHAPTER 14—MATT

By the time Ken reached the spring, clouds were gunmetal gray and the air felt like a freezer. He yanked on his parka and wool hat. Now and then rays of sun inched across the landscape. Though it was only a little past 2:00, he decided it would be a good idea to flash Greg a signal. Might not be another chance. Then he'd find Matt and insist he pack out right away. Morning would be too late. They'd hike home before the snowstorm hit.

Maybe not, he reconsidered. Could lose the trail in the dark. Besides, if they tried to hike home and the storm struck before they got there, they might not find a good campsite. Smarter to climb up to the ridge and build a lean-to on the lee side of the mountain. Get a fire going. Huddle in sleeping bags. Wait out the storm.

He signaled with his mirror and breathlessly waited for a return.

There. Good.

Leaving his pack at the old campsite, he leaped up the granite slabs toward the cave.

"Matt," he yelled, "hey, Matt, it's Ken. Matt, where are you?"

His voice bounced back from the cliffs, a ringing jumble of sounds. Had the guy packed out? Would they get caught in a snowstorm for nothing. Could he make it back up to the ridge before the storm hit?

"Matt! Matt!"

He plunged up the narrow trail, pushing branches aside. The sky grew darker. Everything living disappeared. He shivered and wished he'd worn more clothes under his parka.

Ahead, dry willow leaves rustled.

"Matt, is that you?"

Silence. Then crunching sounds. A moment later, Matt appeared, thinner than six weeks ago, eyes bigger, more deeply set in his face. He glowered at Ken. "Why're you here? You shouldn't've come."

"Look, man, you got to move out."

"What're you talking about?"

"I hiked in to get you."

Matt shook his head. "I'm not going back."

"Once winter sets in you're done for. You won't survive."

"I'll make it."

"No way. I've talked to people, mountain people. They know more about this than you do. Show some sense. Holy cripes, what's the matter with you?"

Matt edged toward him. "Nothing," he said in a low voice.

"Want to get trapped in here? Want to die?"

"Nobody asked you to come in here, kid."

"I won't go back without you," Ken shouted. "Can't you see how stupid this cave thing is? Stop being such a weirdo."

Matt lunged forward and struck Ken's face with his fist.

Ken reeled. He sprawled into a clump of whitethorn, prickles jabbing his neck. His face stung. Blood dripped onto his parka.

Matt yanked Ken to his feet. "Didn't mean to hurt you."

Ken felt dizzy, angry, close to tears.

Matt said, "You shouldn't've come."

"Didn't want you to croak," Ken answered between clenched teeth.

"But to hike in alone—"

"Didn't come alone. Greg's up there on the ridge. Sprained his ankle." Ken shook his head, attempting to clear his fuzzy mind. With the back of his hand he wiped blood from his face onto his jeans. He felt like throwing up. The sun was gone. No way he could signal Greg at 3:30.

Matt stared at the sky.

Ken started down the path.

"You'll get caught in a snowstorm," Matt yelled after him.

"I'll make it."

"With Greg?"

"Sure, sure."

"Not my fault you came in here."

"Forget it," Ken yelled over his shoulder. "Hide in your cave. Freeze your ass off"

"I'll make it," Matt shouted.

"No you won't." Ken turned around and glared at him. "And next spring we'll send in a search party to bury your frozen body."

By the time Ken reached his pack, the sky was iron gray. For a moment, light shone through cloud layers, reflecting golden yellow on the cliffs. Then the granite turned black. Bony-armed willows and veined bushes along the shore stared with a thousand eyes. Ken washed the blood off his face in the spring.

He felt shaky. The cut on his jaw and the pricks on his neck stung as he bathed them. Then they turned numb. He pulled a bandanna from his pack and pressed off the excess water. The bleeding had stopped. He knew he shouldn't have lost his temper with Matt. Realized his approach had been wrong. Wished he'd handled it differently.

Snow began to slip from the sky. Mesmerized, he watched flakes float down. They brought a clean, fresh look to the harsh stone. He heard footsteps scrunching behind him.

It was Matt in a black knit cap and full-length wool coat that looked like army surplus, mittens protruding from a pocket. On his back was an old pack, the same khaki color as the rest of his clothes. "Gonna get you kids home," he said. "Won't be the cause of your freezing to death. That's the only reason I'm leaving."

"I don't need your help." Ken pulled his pack straps over his shoulders and buckled the belt

"You got gloves?" Matt inquired.

Ken yanked them out of his pocket. "Of course."

"After I get you guys home, I'm coming back, understand?"

"I don't care what you do."

They hurried to the trail, Ken in the lead. They started climbing for the crest, feet crunching hollow on the loose rocks. Soon a white blanket covered the mountainside. It grew colder. Snow turned into slippery ice. Scree crackled down the slope like broken glass.

Ken forced himself to keep climbing. His breath shot out in gasps. His chest, face, legs, arms, everything ached. It was hard to see the best spots to dig in his boots. No more shadows; the world had turned flat white. He adjusted his parka hood and wished for ski goggles.

Halfway up, he glanced back at Warren Lake. A blast of wind spun him sideways and threw him against a granite boulder. Matt grabbed his hand. Ken regained his footing and continued climbing.

The wind increased. Each step brought a flood of snow from the sky. They leaned against the mountain, methodically climbing until at last they topped the crest. Stinging, icy blasts tore into them. They staggered. Kneeling down, they shouted, "Greg, Greg...," voices lost to the wind.

The only answer was the hiss of ice against the rocks and the moan of pines below the ridge.

CHAPTER 15—JOE

Business in the coffee shop was slow for Saturday. Velma pushed open the swinging door and barked, "Grilled cheese on wheat. Three slices of onion on the side."

"Only one guy I know stuffs himself with onions," Joe yelled from the kitchen. "that you, Louie?"

"Yeah, it's me," a voice boomed back.

Joe peered over the swinging doors. "How come you're up on the hill?"

It was usually November when Louie appeared on the Summit. He drove a snowplow in the winter for the Division of Highways.

"Check your barometer," said Louie, waving at the instrument on the wall beside the front window. "Dropping fast. Big storm's coming. I'll see action." He gulped his coffee and made a face at the cup. "More cream, Velma. Hey, Joe, make that a fat grilled cheese."

"Bet your life!" Joe crossed the room to peer out the front window.

Louie shoved his thermos across the counter to Velma. "Be a good girl and make a fresh pot for me. The stuff in my cup tastes like mud."

Velma rolled her eyes at the ceiling then reached for the can of coffee.

"When do you think the storm'll hit?" Joe asked Louie.

"In a couple of hours, maybe less."

Joe tapped the barometer. "Should be bells on these things to let you know what's happening."

Louie laughed. "Yeah. Weather guys call this a freak storm. Nobody'll have chains. Cars'll end up in snow banks. Tourists'll huddle in the middle of the freeway like a bunch of sheep." He shook his head in disgust and poured more cream into his coffee. "Yeah, it'll be a mess."

"Lots of snow, huh?"

"Could lay down two feet overnight."

Joe whistled.

Velma said, "Come on, Joe. Get cooking, so I can finish my crossword puzzle."

Joe wrinkled his face at her and returned to the kitchen.

While he grilled the sandwich, he thought about Ken and Greg. He should drive over to Boreal and bring them back now. In a big storm, snow removal equipment would be needed for the highway. The side road to Soda Springs would have to wait. By tomorrow, when he was supposed to pick up the boys, snow could be too deep for his truck to make it to the highway. He arranged onions and pickles around the hot sandwich and punched the bell for Velma.

She whipped in. "About time," she snapped and grabbed the plate.

Joe had important numbers jotted on a piece of cardboard tacked beside the wall phone—sheriff, doctor, fire department volunteer, Bill Kernsey of the ski patrol and Boreal Lodge. Joe dialed Bill's trailer and listened to six rings. Frowning, he hung up and dialed the Lodge.

"Boreal," said a woman's voice.

"Let me talk to Bill Kernsey."

"He's in San Francisco."

"San Francisco?"

"Yeah, but he's on his way back. Called to say he'd try to beat the storm."

Joe shook his head. "I don't get it. What's he doing in San Francisco? He was in his trailer at Boreal this morning."

"Says who?" inquired the woman.

"The kids, the kids."

"What kids? What're you talking about? Bill's been gone all week."

"Impossible. This morning the kids delivered a box of ski equipment to him."

"You're joking."

"No. Two 13-year-old kids. They were in the parking lot. Didn't you see them?"

"Don't know about any kids. Nobody's been at Boreal all day. Oh, wait, at the crack of dawn I heard some kook singing in the parking lot."

"That was me."

"Oh."

"Listen, lady, the kids must be in Bill's trailer and aren't answering the phone. Go and—"

"Nobody's in Bill's trailer. He left his keys with me."

"Then where are the kids?"

"How should I know. Look, the manager's yelling at me."

The line clicked. Joe banged down the receiver and leaned against the wall, wiping his fat hands on his apron.

"Velma," he shouted as he grabbed his jacket, "I'm leaving."

"What?" she yelled from the other room.

He stuck his head through the doorway. "Going to Reede's cabin."

"Reede's cabin?"

"Got to find the kids. So long, Louie. Don't fall in a snowdrift."

Velma cried, "Joe, you can't go now. We're open two more hours."

"Sorry, Velma. You're in charge."

She rushed after him. "Isn't it enough I gotta listen to your fool singing? If you aren't back in fifteen minutes, I'm reporting you."

He balled up his apron and tossed it to her. "Here, keep this warm for me."

"I won't lift a finger to cook," she bellowed as he bounded out the back door. She ran to the doorway and shouted after him, "I'm hired to make coffee, serve food. and clear the counter. That's all. I'm sick of covering for you while you gallivant around." She stood in the doorway, hands on hips, glowering. "You're a lousy bum," she shrieked.

Nicky, the Husky from the gas station, trotted past. The dog refused to look at her. She slammed the door so hard all the pans hanging over the stove rattled.

CHAPTER 16—IAN

At 3:15 in the afternoon, Bill Kernsey turned his truck around in the street so he could park in front of the Reede cabin. Ian sat in the passenger seat. Bill had talked him into returning to the Summit for the weekend. "May need your help on the ski patrol," he'd said.

Ian picked up his books from the rack behind his seat. "How about coming in for some coffee?"

"Okay, a quick cup. Want to get to the summit before bad weather hits." Bill waved at the vehicles parked in front of the house. "Appears you've got company."

"Yeah, that's Joe's truck and..." Ian frowned. "What's Pop's jeep doing here? He should be at the Snow Lab?"

Solemn faces met Ian and Bill as they entered the cabin. Joe told them about the missing boys.

Bill scratched his head. "Last time I saw Ken and Greg was in August. They were returning from a backpack trip and—"

"Wait," said Ian. He scooted up the ladder. "Packs are gone," he shouted and clambered back down the ladder. "They've taken both."

"Where'd the kids go?" cried Joe. He ran to the window as if expecting them to materialize.

"Beats me," said Ian. "You said you took the boys to Boreal. Six trails around there. They could've taken any one."

"Ken should have known better," Mr. Reede said. "Nobody with any sense backpacks up here in October."

Ian could tell by the look in his father's eyes that his angry words were just a front. Ian, too, was afraid. His little kid brother was out there in a soon-to-be blizzard. How could they find him? He noticed how still his mother sat on the couch, hands clasped in her lap. She always stayed cool. Yet he knew fear lay under her calm exterior.

"Kenny acted funny last night," his mother said softly. "Why didn't I pay more attention?"

"They hid everything from me," Joe cried. "All I saw was a big box."

"I saw it, too," said Mr. Reede, pacing the room. "Probably contained their packs. Last night Greg carried it across the porch and crashed down the steps. Sprained his ankle. I should've questioned Greg about the box. Should've found out what was in it. Why didn't I do that?"

"Let's stop blaming ourselves," Mrs. Reede said quietly, "Think about what to do."

Bill went to the window and looked out at the sky.

Mr. Reede continued to pace. "Greg couldn't hike too far with a sprained ankle?"

"They must have a purpose," Ian said. "Otherwise, they wouldn't go this time of year."

"Purpose?" Mr. Reede threw up his arms. "What possible purpose?"

Bill said, "The important thing is to find them. Later we'll figure out why they went."

"Last night," said Mr. Reede, "Kenny and Greg must've crept outside and loaded their packs into that box. They knew I'd never let them go on a harebrained trip." He crossed to the window and stood beside Bill. In a tight voice he said, "It's snowing."

"Go to the Lab, Pop," said Ian. "You'll be needed there. Don't worry. We'll locate the kids."

"How can I work when Kenny's out there?" his father replied in a husky voice. He turned away from the window, his lips trembling.

The jangle of the wall phone in the kitchen made everyone jump.

Ian rushed in and grabbed the receiver. "Hello."

"Who's this?" asked a small female voice on the line.

"Ian Reede."

"Ken's brother?"

"Yeah."

"Well, ah...this is Carolyn Jamison. I...ah...I live down the road."

"I know. I've heard about you."

"Sorry to bother you, but I'm...I'm worried about Ken."

"We are too. Any idea where he is?" Ian heard her catch her breath as if not knowing what to say next. "Carolyn, if you know something..."

"I'm not supposed to tell," she said. "Ken told me not to be a blabbermouth."

"Please, Carolyn, this is serious. If you know where he is... We must find him."

She whispered, "Will the storm get worse?"

"Much worse—a blizzard. And Greg's with him. They could freeze to death."

After a moment of silence, Carolyn said, "They...they hiked into Warren Lake."

"Warren Lake?" Ian looked at his father who stood in the kitchen doorway.

"Yeah, they went in there to save somebody. Don't know who."

"Someone else is at Warren Lake?"

Ian met his father's eyes. "They hiked in to get somebody."

Carolyn cleared her throat. "Ken said if he didn't come back by Sunday afternoon, to call you then, but with the snowstorm coming, I thought maybe I should.... He'll be okay, won't he?"

"Hope so. It's a good thing you called."

"Please let me know—" Her voice faltered. "Call me when you find him."

"Sure. Thanks, Carolyn." Ian hung up the receiver and walked back into the living room. His father was at the window. Ian gave him a reassuring pat on the shoulder. "Most likely, they're on their way home now. Ken's learned a lot about the wilderness."

His father shook his head. "Not enough."

Bill said, "Ian, get hold of the Sheriff's Office in Truckee. Here's the number. Explain the situation."

"Okay." Ian ran back to the phone and dialed.

Joe sprang for the front door, yelling. "Come on. Let's get the kids out."

"Sit down, Joe," Bill commanded. "You can't just dash off into the wilderness. You have to make plans."

Joe pounded his head with his fists, then perched on the edge of the flowered chair, mumbling, "If I'd had any idea, I'd never've taken them to Boreal. Said they were delivering ski gear to you. Thought it was odd carrying it in a junky, taped-up box. I should've known better."

Bill yanked a small notebook from his back pocket. "Got a list of names here, fellows living in the area, all Ski Patrol members."

He copied the names and numbers on another page and tore it off, handing it to Mr. Reede.

"Want me to phone them?" Mr. Reede asked.

"Yeah, line up three or four to act as a backup team. Tell them to meet me at Boreal right away."

"I'll call from the Lab." Mr. Reede briefly clasped hands with his wife, then hurried out the front door.

Ian held the phone receiver. "Bill, someone at the Sheriff's office wants to talk to you. I'll get on my gear." He headed for the loft ladder.

"Kernsey here," Bill said into the receiver.

A crisp voice on the other end said, "This is Lieutenant Jorgensen. What's all the fuss, Bill?"

"A party of three at Warren Lake: the young Reede boy and Greg Browsky."

"Greg Browsky?"

"You know him. Lives in Truckee, Gus's nephew?"

"Right, I remember him. His folks were killed two years ago in that car accident. Who's the third person?"

"Don't know."

"Surely they'll be out before the storm hits."

"Already hit up here, Lieutenant. Snowing heavily. Wind's picking up. Most likely blizzard conditions at higher elevations.."

The lieutenant sighed. "All right, Bill, I'm putting you in charge. Arrange for rescue if you think it's necessary."

"I do. First, I'll send in a 'hasty search' party."

"Names."

"Ian Reede and myself, and I hope to get Jess Lowry, the snow ranger."

"Saw him in Truckee five minutes ago. I'll contact him."

"Tell him to meet me at Boreal."

"I will, and since we're short at the office, I'll ask Highway Patrol to send a squad car to the Summit Rest Area."

"Good idea. I'll keep in touch." Bill hung up.

"What can I do?" asked Joe. "If I don't do something, I'll go crazy."

"Know how to operate a radio system?"

"Bet your life!"

"Then, come with us to Boreal. We'll set up a station."

Ian climbed down the ladder. He wore waterproof pants and parka, a knit cap and cross-country ski boots. Clipped to his pocket zipper was a pair of gloves; pushed on top of his head, yellow goggles.

His mother came out of the downstairs bedroom with his father's backpack. "Kenny's never been caught in a snowstorm," she said in a shaky voice as she handed Ian the pack. "I don't think he'll know what to do."

Ian nodded grimly and hurried to the back porch for his skis and poles. "Don't worry, Mom," he called back. "We'll find them."

"I need a job," his mother insisted, looking close to tears. "What can I do?"

Bill said, "Stay by the phone. Relay any calls that come in. Here's my number."

Ian kissed his mother on the cheek and hurried for the front door.

101

Bill said to him, "When we get to Boreal, gather the first-aid gear. Posted in the patrol room is a list of what's necessary. Meanwhile, I'll change clothes, get the ropes, wands, and food. We'll start out on foot, carrying the skis on our backs. Go that way as long as possible."

Joe stood on the front porch, his arms raised. "Look at it snow," he cried. "Those crazy kids."

CHAPTER 17—BLIZZARD

Ken struggled against the wind. Blasts of icy needles stung his face. He rubbed his frosted eyelashes and yanked his parka hood strings tighter. Pulling off a glove, he tried to tie the strings. His fingers wouldn't work. He yanked the glove back on and pounded his hands together. Beside him Matt loomed like a giant snowman.

Got to get out of the wind, Ken thought. Get out or we'll freeze. Find shelter. Think about Greg later. Matter of survival.

He remembered a lodgepole pocket below the ridge. Beating on Matt's back, he pointed in the direction. He squinted for his bearings and inched to the edge of the saddle, careful of his footing, afraid of plunging over the cliff. As he peered back to make certain Matt followed, granular snow hit his face in a stinging cloud.

Keep moving, he told himself. Head for the lee side.

At last they were below the ridge. Gusts swirled the snow around them, but the mountain and the trees broke the force of the wind. Not a whiteout like at the top.

Unsure which way to go, Ken stood there a few moments. He pictured Greg's face. Might never see him again. Shouldn't have asked him to come. Ken's stomach churned and he swallowed hard. Matt batted him on the shoulder.

Ken nodded and pushed Greg's face away. Can't lose focus, he told himself. Got to keep moving. Find shelter. He circled a mass of rocks and brush wedged in under trees. Ahead stood a fractured boulder overhanging a flat area. Crawl underneath the ledge, he thought. Find dried pine needles in crevices. Pull off dead lodgepole limbs. Start a fire. Good thing I took some matches.

He shoved back a branch. At first he didn't comprehend what he saw. From the boulder, a tarp reached out for about a yard. Slanted and staked at the bottom, it stretched shoulder high between the trees. He grabbed Matt's arm and pointed. Then, in a flash, he understood. "Greg?" he yelled, scrambling around to the open side. "Greg?"

From the gloom a voice chattered, "A-about-t-time."

Ken threw off his pack and dug in it till he found the flashlight. He pressed the switch. It really was Greg. There he was, curled up in his sleeping bag, crouched against the base of the boulder. In front of him was a pile of dead branches and the tinderbox open, matches spilled out.

"It's Greg," Ken yelled.

Matt, fell to his knees and waved for him to hurry ahead. Ken leaned the flashlight against a rock, crawled in under the tarp and squeezed Greg's shoulders.

"Good old bonehead," he cried. "Afraid I wouldn't find you. Thought you might have started back."

"W-wouldn't d-do a d-dumb thing like that," Greg said.

Matt scooted onto the ledge and shook the snow off his shoulders. With a grimace, he took off his gloves and blew on his fingers. "I'll build a fire." He tossed the tinder onto the branches and gathered up the matches. Soon flames crackled and popped and smoke escaped through the air hole in the tarp.

It took nearly an hour for Greg to warm up enough to stop shaking. By that time, snow had bunkered around the tarp, muffling the sounds of the wind. Matt and Ken took turns feeding the fire. They huddled in their sleeping bags, bunched together, Greg in the middle. They sipped Matt's hot mint tea while outside the blizzard took over the mountain, hissing, crying, moaning like a distant wild creature.

Ken was surprised at the change that had come over Matt. Gone was the angry, isolated weirdo. Perhaps the necessity of working together to survive had brought it about. Or was this the real guy, the other one only a protective shield? Whatever, Ken felt he now had a bond with Matt. Not as strong as with Greg, honed over time, but a bond nonetheless.

Greg said to Ken, "When it started to snow, I figured you wouldn't stay at the lake over night. Knew you'd come back up. Hoped you'd be smart enough to head for trees on the lee side. After I staked the tarp and dragged in these branches, I tried to start a fire. But my fingers shook too much."

"How's the ankle?" Matt asked.

"Took off the shoe and bandage—too tight. Then couldn't get them on again."

"Looks really swollen."

"I wrapped my ankle in plastic bags. Barely managed to pull my double socks up over." He shifted his position, bringing his feet closer to the fire. "Saw more dead branches below the rocks. Didn't try to get them. Afraid I'd fall. And I was so cold. Couldn't even hold a match. Just curled up and prayed you'd come in time."

"What a blizzard!" Matt said, pulling his cap lower over his ears.

"I've seen worse," said Ken. "One winter 50 feet fell on Mount Lincoln. We had to dig our cabin out of the snow—drifts piled up to the roof."

"You're kidding!"

"No, that's why we came to get you."

"I could've survived."

"I doubt it."

Matt glanced at the snow covering the entrance and sighed. "Well, maybe not." Briefly he met Ken's eyes. "Can't believe you hiked in just to get me." He crawled out of his bag. "Come on, let's bring up more firewood. Got a rope?"

"Sure."

"How about if we tie it to a tree? I'll climb down the bank, tie on dead branches and you pull them up."

"Good idea. Let's go. Snow's still soft enough at the opening to push our way out."

While Greg fried Spam and heated water for instant noodles, Matt and Ken hauled up three loads.

After supper Matt said, "You guys sleep. I'll tend the fire. Get my shut-eye in the a.m."

Soon after Greg lay down, his snores blended with the wind, wailing through the trees and whistling around the smoke vent.

Burrowed in his bag, Ken tried to clear his mind of nagging fears. He could see his parent's faces—frantic—not knowing where he was. Would he ever see them again? It hit him that he might not survive. That his life might end here on this ledge. A flash of cold swept through him.

What if we run out of wood and can't find any more? he thought. How much food have we got? Matt has dried fish, prunes, marshmallows and mint for tea. Along with our supplies, enough to eat for maybe five days. But sometimes blizzards last longer than that.

He imagined himself starving. Although he'd never liked prunes, he had the temptation to leap up and wolf one down. He remembered that first time when his father drove the family up to their mountain home, and he'd imagined himself lying dead on an isolated cliff—nobody but the wind knew where he was.

Stop thinking about this, he told himself. Come on, get your mind in another track.

"Matt," he whispered, "how'd you find out about Warren Lake?"

"Heard a couple of guys talking at school. Said they were lucky to find this lake with so few campers around. I bought a topo map and checked the location. After school let out in June, grabbed my pack and hitched a ride to the summit. Planned only to stay the summer. Discovered the cave and decided to stay longer. Quiet, peaceful, relaxing. Birds, squirrels, picas, marmots—all the animals were my friends." He looked sideways at Ken. "Sounds wacky, doesn't it?"

"No." Ken remembered the time he tried to pet a deer, thinking it was his friend. Although his father and Ian had laughed at him, his mother had given him a hug. He swallowed hard. "Your family must be worried about you."

"Nobody worries about me. Last year I camped all summer in the Trinity Alps."

"My brother's hiked there. Isn't it in Northern California?"

"Yeah."

"I read about it in a magazine. Sounds like a neat place."

"Peaceful, too." Matt pulled the bag tighter around his shoulders. "Came home two months later. My mother didn't know I ever went."

"Maybe she didn't want to pry into your life."

"That wasn't it. She's got too many problems. My stepfather owns a construction company in Sacramento. Both work there. She runs the office. They're not home much. Just as well. When they are, he sits in front of the TV and drinks till he's plastered. Ends up fighting with my mother. Usually hits her. Then she locks herself in the bedroom and yells through the door. Once she threatened to burn the house down. Don't know why they stay together."

His eyes narrowed. "I hated the guy from the start. When he came to live with us four years ago, I tried to stop him from hitting her. He beat me up. Three times he beat me up. Last time I looked bad. Skipped school. What a mean bastard! After that, whenever they started yelling, I went outside. Sat on the back steps. Tried not to listen. Pretended it was a lousy radio program. Tuned everything out. Told myself it had nothing to do with me."

He stared at the fire. "My little sister used to cry when they went at it. At 14, she started staying away all night." He shook his head. "Sometimes what happened didn't seem real. Like I'd stumbled onto another planet with all these strange creatures walking around. Each day my mother left money on the counter for my sister and me—lunch and dinner money. I ate at McDonald's. Saved a little dough for camping trips. One day I found out my sister used her money for drugs. Only 14, and she got into meth."

His voice softened. "She used to be a sweet kid. I remember when she was nine. She wore a pink dress on Sundays. Once she won an Easter rabbit in a grocery store raffle, a real rabbit. Got a photograph of her in that pink dress. She's holding the bunny. Looks so happy. Two weeks later somebody stole her rabbit. She thought it would find a way to get back. All night she sat by the empty hutch and cried. I offered her my skates. No, she wanted her rabbit. Said I'd buy her anything she wanted. She only wanted the rabbit she'd won on her own.

"Now all she thinks about is getting drugs. Only 14." He sighed, reached back for another stick and poked it into the fire. "Tried to talk to her about it. She wouldn't listen. Think she's glad when I'm gone. That way she can have my counter money."

Matt stopped talking and stared at the fire. Ken wanted to say something that could help, but everything he thought about sounded silly. He hoped Matt would know how he felt.

"I'm dropping' out of school," Matt continued. "No good, anyway. Won't help me with my life. Not going back home either." He rubbed his face hard. "Didn't want to stay in that cave forever. Just didn't know what else to do."

Matt looked at Ken in as if he hadn't seen him before. "Geez, shouldn't have poured all this on you."

"Glad you did, Matt. It's good to hear you talk about your problems." Ken pressed his lips together. "Wish I knew what to say. Something to help."

"Don't need anybody's help."

"Everybody needs it when life gets tough."

Matt looked away. "Go to sleep, Ken. You've had a tough day."

CHAPTER 18—WAITING

Ken lay awake in his warm bag, his knit hat still pulled over his ears, thinking about Matt, wondering where the guy might go and what might happen to him. He felt lucky having people who cared about him, wished he could let them know he was all right, hoped his mother and father would understand why he had to make this trip.

His thoughts hazed. He had a vague notion this was how Stubby must feel at the start of hibernation. Before dozing off, he saw images of his family and Joe and Carolyn—all part of one picture, faces fading into each other.

Snow built up in deep drifts around the shelter until the wailing disappeared, replaced by a hollow sound over the smoke hole like someone blowing on top of an empty bottle.

Greg groaned in his sleep. Ken raised up and said, "You okay?"

"My toes," Greg mumbled and dropped back into snoring.

Matt pulled the bottom of Greg's bag closer to the fire and added another piece of wood to the flames.

In the morning, while Matt slept, Ken insisted on examining Greg's sprained ankle. Gingerly, Greg rolled down his socks and took off the plastic bags. Ken felt the black and blue areas, Greg wincing with each touch.

"Not as swollen as yesterday," Ken said. "Any feeling in your foot?"

"Yeah, in most of it."

"How about your toes?"

"Not sure."

"Well, let me see them."

"Don't want to take my socks off."

"You have to. Your toes may be frostbitten."

Greg clenched his teeth. He eased off the double pair of socks, exposing a badly swollen big toe, pink, beginning to blister. The other toes were white and waxy.

"Can you move them?" Ken asked.

"Just the big one. It's on fire. Can't feel the others."

Ken touched the icy toes. Abruptly, he climbed out of his bag and knelt. He lifted the bottom edges of his two jackets, then pulled aside his shirt, exposing midriff skin. "Put your foot here," he commanded, pointing to his stomach.

"That's ridiculous."

"Just do it. You've got to get feeling back in your toes."

"No!"

"Yes!"

Gently but firmly, Ken set Greg's foot against his stomach, determined not to shiver from the cold. He covered the foot with his shirt and both parkas. He pretended not to feel the penetrating ice of the toes, pretended to study his backpacking checklist, though now his concentration was on how they could make it home once the storm was over. He knew Greg wouldn't be able to hike out.

What if I used his backpack as a stretcher? he asked himself.

No, he thought. Aluminum frames aren't strong enough.

I could lash the packs together as a sled.

Not a good idea. Ice and snow would rip off the covers.

How about cutting down two saplings and roping the tarp between them?

Yeah, that's the best bet. Soon as the blizzard quits, I'll find the saplings.

But, what if the storm continues for days? We might never make it out. Trapped, frozen stiff, eaten by wolves and vultures.

He remembered his daydreams about dangerous adventures, imagining Gypsy a cougar ready to leap on him from a jagged cliff. How silly those fantasies seemed. Right now, he'd give anything to be home again—to lie on his sheepskin rug and watch the sky darken between lodgepole branches; to scratch Gypsy's ears and listen to her purr; to eat his mother's apricot pie.

He held Greg's foot against his stomach till he complained about pain in his toes. "That's a good sign," Ken said. He rewrapped Greg's ankle and helped slip the plastic bags and socks back on. After adding more wood to the fire, he climbed back into his sleeping bag, shivering a bit, glad for the warmth. He cut his share from an apple and ate it in little bites, relishing each piece.

Greg fell asleep, no snoring now. Matt still slept. It grew quiet, wonderfully quiet—the only sound, the crackling fire. Slowly, it dawned on Ken that he no longer heard the wind. Peering up through the smoke hole, he glimpsed daylight.

A lull in the storm, he thought. I'll dig out through the drift. Get a little exercise. See if any saplings are nearby for the stretcher.

He emerged into a white world. The wind was gone. Snow fell in large flakes. With each step, he sank above his knees. Canyon drifts would be six feet deep, he guessed—maybe more. Moving through them would be difficult. Tough enough here. A group of partially submerged saplings stood nearby. He unsheathed his knife and hacked away, managing to cut two. Might not be strong enough, he worried, and left the saplings outside the shelter. Lace fringes hung from the lodgepole branches, and tree trunks, with blankets of snow built up around their bases, stood out in sharp contrast to the white sky.

No way to locate more wood for a fire, he thought as he studied the landscape.

Shoving fear aside, he climbed on top of the rock shelf and plowed his way up through a waist-high drift to the saddle. Wind had swept the top clean, and flakes were starting to whiten it again. He leaned against a rock and stared far down at Warren Lake, a gray pearl in a white bowl.

Gradually, blue sky appeared in the south. A patch. Then more. Clouds parted. At last the sun broke though and lit the ridges golden, touching snowflakes until they looked like hot coals. As the clouds raced north, more and more blue appeared. Magically, the snow stopped falling.

Ken let out a whoop. "Blizzard's over," he cried.

Matt's startled face appeared at the edge of the shelf. "What's wrong?"

"Hey man, come up here. Have a look."

Matt struggled out and plodded up toward the saddle. He blinked, his eyes red and puffy.

"See," Ken shouted. He lifted his arms to the increasingly blue sky. "Blizzard's over. We made it through the storm."

They thumped each other on the shoulders, yelling for joy. Then Ken saw three dots moving on the other side of the bowl. "Look," he shouted, and they thumped some more, waved their arms, shouted louder.

Greg's muffled voice called out, "Quit that racket. How's a guy supposed to sleep?"

"Storm's over," Ken called down to him. "Skiers headed our way. We're going home."

Matt's smile disappeared.

Ken touched him on the shoulder. "Don't worry, Matt. We'll figure out something for you. Good things are bound to happen."

"Doubt it." Matt screwed up one side of his mouth. "You should've left me in there."

Ken swallowed hard. "Aren't you glad we all survived?"

Matt stared down at Warren Lake. "Glad you and Greg did," he said in a husky voice. Turning away, he started back to the shelter.

CHAPTER 19—RESCUE

"Rescue One calling Boreal Base. Boreal, come in—over," Bill Kernsey said into the radio. He sat in the shelter beside Ian while Jess Lowry, the Snow Ranger, applied sterile dressings to Greg's damaged foot.

"How do you feel?" Jess asked as he finished wrapping the foot and ankle.

"Lousy," Greg replied.

"Pills should kick in soon."

Joe's voice crackled over the radio, "Rescue One, this is Boreal Base. Over."

"Joe, we found the boys," said Bill.

"Hurray! They okay?"

"Ken's in top shape, but Greg's got a sprained ankle and frostbitten toes."

"Bad?"

"Won't run races for a while."

"Tell him I'm sorry."

"He heard you, Joe."

"Good. And tell Ken he better not keep secrets from me any more."

"Okay."

"Where are you?"

"Four miles past where we bivouacked last night in the whiteout. On the eastern side of the ridge above Warren Lake, approximately thirty feet south of the trail to the saddle. Ken's waiting on the ridge. Repeat our location."

Joe did.

Bill turned to Jess. "Think we need a helicopter for Greg?"

"No—not a life or death situation. Besides, locating a chopper, getting it here and loading Greg into it, might take more time than for us to bring him out. And Gus'd have to pay for it. Course, it's your operation, Bill."

"How about Greg's toes?"

"He's got feeling in all of them now. A matter of warding off infection. Another ten minutes and the pills should help with the pain."

Bill said to Greg, "Can you handle a toboggan ride?"

Greg nodded and produced a faint smile.

"Hey, Bill," Joe said, coming on again, "Rescue Two just passed Raccoon Canyon."

A loud buzzing filled the radio till Joe's voice broke through again. "Got two guys with snowmobiles. They want to come help."

"Appreciate their offer," said Bill, "but tell them to stay away. Vibrations might trigger avalanches. On the way in, saw two cornices ready to fall."

"Okay. Sheriff's office wants third party's name."

"Matt Harley." Bill glanced at Matt, huddled under the rock behind the fire. "Refuses to give a home address. Claims he's 18. Might be a runaway."

A minute later Joe said, "Sheriff says he'll check it out."

Bill said to Ian, "When toboggans get here, strap Greg to one and Matt to the other."

Matt half rose. "Don't strap me to anything."

"Want to ski out? That's what Ken's gonna do. Rescue Two's bringing in extra pairs."

"I'm walking."

"Not in these deep drifts. Nobody could walk out of here."

Matt sighed and sank back down, his face buried between hunched knees. "Don't know how to ski," he muttered.

More static on the line, and then Joe said, "Greg's uncle and an ambulance are waiting for him. And I got news for Ken. His friend

Domino's at the trailhead. When he heard about the kids in the blizzard, he drove up from Auburn. Don't know how he missed the highway closure at Nyak. That old guy must know every back road in the Sierra."

Bill chuckled and looked at Ian. "Anything you want to say?"

Ian took the receiver. "Tell Pop my little brother's become an experienced mountain man."

"Always thought he was," Joe replied. "Good you're getting out today. Another storm's predicted for tomorrow."

"Hope it won't jump in sooner."

"It won't. I've been singing all morning. If that storm gets crazy ideas, I got enough lung power to blow it to China."

"Keep singing, Joe."

"Bet your life."

Ken's head appeared through the branches. "Four people and two toboggans are coming. Greg, they're crossing the bee field."

"Joe," Bill called into the radio. "Rescue One in sight. Over."

"Roger." said Joe. "You guys pack up and leave that place to the wind. Out."

Good weather held for the trek home. For safety they detoured around two possible avalanche sections. Once, Jess narrowly missed getting buried when a cornice collapsed. Another time, when Matt's toboggan tipped over into a drift, it took three of the rescuers to dig it out and set it right.

A few feet from the trailhead, Bill untied Matt and let him plow out on his own.

A crowd was waiting—newspaper reporters, photographers, a television crew, relatives, friends and gawkers. Also, two Highway Patrol cars and an ambulance.

The police officers reported no missing-person bulletin filed on Matt. They interrogated him. He continued to say he was 18 and claimed he had no home address. After listening to a heated exchange between Matt and a patrolman, Domino stepped up.

"Son, what do you think about horses?"

"Never been around them," Matt replied belligerently.

"You like animals?"

"Yeah, they're my best friends."

"That's a good start. Shows you got sense." Domino scratched his scraggly beard. "I could use an extra hand. Don't have much to offer, but it's better'n a cold cave. These police fellas know where I am if they gotta see you again."

Ken said to Matt, "Domino's a great guy. Keeps his horses down in Auburn every winter, but for the rest of the year he runs the pack-horse stable in Summit Valley. That's near where I live.

The old man's face creased into a warm smile. "Yep, Ken and I've been buddies for quite a spell."

Matt studied Domino sideways. "Might as well try it." He glanced at Ken. "Thanks for your help, kid. Maybe I'll see you next summer."

He picked up his pack and walked off with the old man toward his truck.

CHAPTER 20—GOODBYE

"Hi, blabbermouth," Ken said with a grin. He stood in Carolyn's front doorway late the next morning.

"You didn't go to school today," she said.

"Mom let me sleep in."

"Glad you're safe. Did I do wrong? I mean, was telling Ian a bad thing to do?"

"You probably saved my life."

"I don't believe that. When your father phoned last night, he said you could've handled the blizzard for a week."

"No kidding. He said that? Told me I was lucky to be alive."

Ken was surprised he didn't feel more elated. For so long he had wanted his father's approval. Now he was glad to have it—pleased, relieved—but it didn't seem as important.

"How come all these suitcases are out here?" he asked, looking around the room. "You planning on going someplace?"

"Would you like an apple? We got peanuts in that can over there."

"Just finished breakfast." He sat at the table. A sense of unease spread over him. "Why are you standing over there. Don't you want to hear how I made it through the blizzard?

"Of course I do." She sat across from him.

"That's better." He saw her loose-leaf binder on the table—*Plant Specimens from Donner Summit* printed on the cover. "Been working on your flower book?"

"No. I brought it out because..." She fingered the book. "Because I thought you might like to borrow it."

He looked up quickly. "Something's wrong, isn't it?"

She faced the window. He heard a person walking around in the other room. A floorboard squeaked. A drawer opened and closed.

"You're moving away, aren't you?" he said softly. "That's it. That's why you're upset."

She nodded.

"Want to talk about it?"

"No."

He reached across the table and took her hands—incredibly soft, yet cold and trembling. He cradled them in his.

Gradually her trembling stopped. Her hands relaxed. She continued to stare out the window.

Finally she said, "We're leaving today."

He squeezed her hands."Want to tell me where you're gonna go?"

"Have to go to a hospital, a special kind...it's in Seattle."

"Yeah, well, okay," he murmured, not knowing what else to say.

She looked at him, a touch of defiance in her eyes. "I'm going to the hospital because my health is, well...it's getting worse." She cleared her throat. "Should've told you this before, but I was afraid if you knew you wouldn't come back. You see, what I have is...leukemia."

"I knew that."

"You did?"

"Yeah." He cleared his throat. "I've known it for quite a while."

"Really?"

"Yeah." He swallowed hard. "It's good you're going to the hospital. Doctors'll make you well, and while you're there I'll write to you."

"You will?"

"Sure thing. And you'll be back before you know it."

Mrs. Jamison appeared from the bedroom, holding a coat.

Carolyn pulled her hands away and pushed the binder toward Ken. "Keep it for me."

"Yeah, I'll..." He couldn't seem to find words. "Yeah...I'll...I'll take good care of it," he managed to say.

Saying goodbye to Carolyn was the hardest thing Ken had ever done. He stood for a moment at the foot of the path before he had the courage to turn around and wave to her. She sat at the window, waving back, smiling.

Already the sun had melted some of the snow. Rivulets ran down the freshly plowed street, empty of cars and people. The crisp air smelled of wood smoke from cabin fires. Lake Van Norden spread out to the east like a sheet of silver.

With the flower book tucked under an arm, he climbed the Soda Springs Ski Hill. The slope was mushy. Soon his jeans were wet to his knees. Every muscle in his body ached from yesterday's hike, yet climbing the hill seemed necessary.

From the top he looked north to Castle Peak, remote, cold, rising black above a white shroud. Snow ribbons clung to its steep face. Far to the right was the first ridge he had crossed on the way to Warren Lake. Beside him hung the red chairlift. Below, Carolyn's window stood out from every other window.

The hospital will make her well, he told himself. She'll get better. And when she comes back, we'll hike up here. I'll show her the lichens on the volcanic rocks. She'll sit under the Jeffrey pine and ride the ski chair. We'll pull up bunches of wild onions for a stew.

But what if she doesn't come back? He pressed his lips together and swallowed hard. At his feet a crumpled tin can dazzled in the sun. He grabbed the can and hurled it down the slope. It hit a rock, bounced with a clink and dropped into the snow.

Clutching the flower book, he sank down under the old Jeffrey pine and leaned against the trunk. He wiped his runny nose on the back of a sleeve. His hands were cold. He'd forgotten his gloves.

A mountain chickadee called from a limb above him.

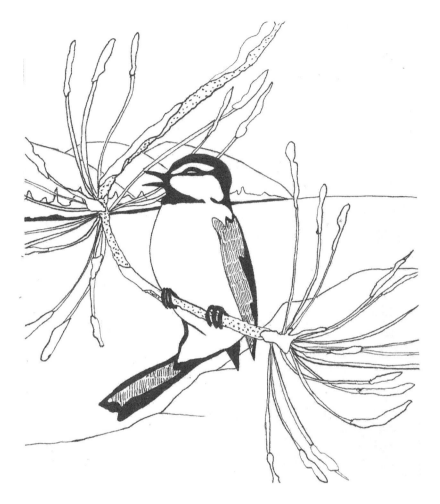

The bird hopped around, hung upside down, investigated the wood and pecked for a bug. Then it flew off to rejoin its flock in the lodgepole forest.

Most animals move down to safer elevations, Ken thought. Or hibernate. Chickadees stay though. They know how to survive. And this old tree. He touched the rough bark of the twisted Jeffrey pine. It's learned how to face the worst and survive.

A tenor voice broke through the cold air, the song filling the valley: "You shall walk where only the wind has walked before." It was Joe at the coffee shop. He sang in English, rare for him. His voice rose high and vibrant. "And when all music is stilled, you shall hear the singing of the stream...."

Ken hugged the flower book to his chest and started down the hill, tramping out fresh tracks. He retrieved the tin can and dumped it in the garbage bin behind the lodge. Today he didn't feel like visiting Joe. Maybe tomorrow.

Around the corner of the ski shop, he took a long look at Carolyn's cabin. An icy gust hit his face. Dark clouds were massing to the south—another storm building. He pulled the red wool cap down over his ears. Holding the book tight under his arm, he shoved his cold hands into his pockets.

He walked home beside the road, humming the music Joe had been singing. Maybe he didn't have the tune right, but just trying made him feel better.

THE END

ACKNOWLEDGMENTS

Many thanks to the following:

Nancy Rekow for editing the book;
Kathryn Keve, Larry Fowler, Brett Gadbois and Mike Smith for making helpful suggestions;
Son, Mikael, for contributing illustrations in memory of his brother;
Husband, Grant, for listening to chapters and reminiscing while we drank 5 a.m. coffee in bed.

Made in the USA
San Bernardino, CA
12 February 2015